James Prior

Three Shots from a Popgun

James Prior

Three Shots from a Popgun

ISBN/EAN: 9783337017835

Printed in Europe, USA, Canada, Australia, Japan

Cover: Foto ©Thomas Meinert / pixelio.de

More available books at **www.hansebooks.com**

THREE SHOTS

FROM A

POPGUN.

BY

JAMES PRIOR.

London:

REMINGTON AND CO.,

5, ARUNDEL STREET, STRAND, W.C.

1880.

CONTENTS.

———

THREE
SHOTS FROM A POPGUN.

WISE OR OTHERWISE.

CHAPTER I.

GOOD-DAY to you, madam; and good-day to you, sir. Welcome to Nottingham. Have you any engagements, or may I hope you will accept my company for a stroll this sunny September afternoon? You will! I am greatly honoured. You have not seen much of the town, I daresay? As I thought; you have seen the Market-place pump and the Town Hall, and that is all. Well, be good enough, without more ceremony, to follow me, and I will show you a better sight.

Puff! Now we are out of the streets, and can speak and be heard. This broad avenue that you see before you is the Queen's Walk. These buildings that hedge it on every hand

B

are the Meadows, so called because once, thirty years ago, there were meadows here green all the year, save in the springtime, when they were blue over with crocuses. Ah, if it were only thirty years ago! And why not, if we choose to have it so, and for an hour clear our memory of all the dust and rubbish that has been accumulating these thirty years? Let it be thirty years ago now, dear companions. Pardon me, I am too soon familiar. Let the Queen and all of us be thirty years younger to-day; and let us see here nothing but what we might have seen thirty years ago.

So we are now at the end of the Walk, and by the banks of the Trent. This thing that fronts us is not an iron bridge, but a rustic ferry—Wilford Ferry, worked by one man's arm. We enter the boat, and cross in company with a milk-cart, a Nottingham stockinger, with fishing-rod and mat basket in hand, and a pair of sweethearts bound for Clifton Grove.

Safely landed with a bump! The village close at hand, almost hidden by innumerable elms is Wilford. However, we will not enter it now, but will turn to the right by this White House Inn, making for the church, whose tower and spire you can see in spite of the trees.

Allow me, ladies, to assist you over this high stile. Now here we are, with nothing but a low barrier between us and the church-yard that grave-haunted Kirke White loved. But before you enter, sit down and admire the scene.

It is scarcely spoilt even now, though green fields are blotted out with red brick, and a colliery belches smoke on the opposite bank of the river. But yes, I remember, we are at thirty years ago. Northward, beyond the Trent, see a broad sweep of rich meadow-land, besprinkled with trees, and bordered by pleasant hills, from which to our left rise the heights of Wollaton, clad with verdure, through which peeps the white face of a soli-tary mansion. To the right of these lie the houses and gentler slopes of Lenton; and next the bluff on which stands Nottingham, its two most prominent headlands crowned, the one by the Castle, the other by St. Mary's tower.

Further still, and faintly seen through the September haze, Sneinton Church sits on its own hill, like a little St. Mary's. Last of all the bold Rough Hill, covered with wood, flings round to our flank, and cuts off the view.

And all the while the river, placid and full in this autumn time, rolls swiftly at our feet, and the breeze flutters the old elms that overhang us, and the birds that inhabit them fly busily in and out of doors.

We have loitered here long enough, and our seat is none of the comfortablest; let us over the stile and into the churchyard, which is closely begirt on every side with great elms.

But hush! We have company here beside the sheep that browse on the graves—a young gentleman sitting on the low stone wall that skirts the river. As I happen to know him pretty well, allow me to introduce him to you, ladies and gentlemen; that is, mentally, for I would not disturb him at this moment for a hundred pounds. Mr. Humphrey Denton, ladies and gentlemen; a young man aged twenty-one years, and of much promise; for that is the promising age. And the time for fulfilment—when? Will it be ever and ever to-morrow? For oh! if we could only live to-morrow, how good should we become—aye, the worst of us; and what good we should do, even the idlest of us.

But all this is nothing to Mr. Humphrey Denton, who is twenty-one, and still sitting thoughtfully on the wall. If we could only draw near enough to hear him think! Do not you catch something like this?—

"What a voice she has! and what eyes! and what an honest heart! And what— If ever a man was haunted I am; and by no evil spirits—crossed in every path by pair of bright eyes and a supernatural voice. What a marvel it is, the world of music that one little throat includes! Such larks ought not to be private; they should be caught and set in public to sing for the commonwealth's re-generation. All but Polly! A flock of such birds would preach evil out of our thorough-fares, for who would act basely or give the world over-much regard while heaven was so apparently sounding near him?"

A very strange young fellow! And it is

well he only thinks his wild notions; for, did he utter them, he would earn a foolish name. But see! ever on the alert, he catches a glimpse through the hedge of something womanly coming along the path by which we entered. He is off his seat in a twinkling, and gains the cover of one of the church tower's deep buttresses.

Presently a girl shows herself within a few yards of him; tall, shapely, and dark-eyed, carrying a large bundle in a blue checked wrapper. Evidently a work-girl, though decently, even gracefully, clad.

The young man, taken so vigilantly unawares, will not notice her until she has well caught sight of him. When he turns, and says with an air of pleasurable surprise—

" Why, good afternoon, Polly ! "

Her face flushes, until she looks like one of those roses that we love; but whether with pleasure or pain, you could not decide; perhaps both.

" Good afternoon, Mr. Humphrey."

" As I have met you," he says again, " I have something to tell you. Sit down and take a little rest meanwhile."

"I must not loiter, sir," Polly answers; "I was delayed half an hour yesterday."

"But my news concerns Mike."

"What is it?" she asks, more eagerly.

He motions his hand towards the wall on which he has been sitting, and says in a business-like manner—

"Sit down then, while I tell you."

Being anxious to hear, she cannot refuse to fulfil the conditions. She sits down, though uneasily, and he beside her.

"I've just heard that the cricket committee have decided to play Mike all next season."

"Oh, thank you, Mr. Humphrey!" cries Polly, starting up. "How proud father will be! and how glad I am!"

"You are not keeping your contract, Polly," says Mr. Humphrey, pointing to her empty seat; and she sits down again obediently, for there may be more to hear.

"I knew," he continues, "that they would play him. What splendid cuts he makes!"

"And what drives, too!" cries the enthusiastic Polly.

" And what a steady defence for so young a player ! "

" And his fielding, too, so good ! "

" Do you remember when he threw Leggy out at Sutton in Ashfield ? "

" And when he caught Spooner out at Burton Joyce ? "

" And his score of a hundred and thirty-six against the Bumpers ? "

" And ninety-eight not out for the Screw-drivers ? "

" How is it," says Humphrey, suddenly changing key, tempo, and tone, " how is it that you could sing ' Old Robin Gray ' last night so feelingly ? You never had the misfortune to marry him, nor yet any younger and less estimable man."

" If I had," answers Polly, with an archly-subdued smile, " I fear I should have found it nothing to sing about."

" How I pitied you in your heap of woes. My grief rose at each fresh disaster—your father's accident, the theft of your cow, your mother's sickness, until when Old Robin Gray came a-courting you, I could have wept."

Polly replies—

" You are laughing at me because I was so earnest in play."

" Nay, I was myself too earnest for play, and felt the misery more than the art. My pity fell like the rain, without thinking of the need."

Polly twists her head away, and kicks a stone with a shapely foot, as she replies deliberately—

" You should have gathered up your pity as it fell, and saved it against the need."

" Well, with the remnants I will be very pitiful to some one, Polly, for your sake."

" I must go," she says with a jerk, making to rise.

" One moment more. Does it not make you happy to sit here at ease, feeling the sun's warmth in the shade? with the birds chirruping, the lazy breeze (if this is a breeze and not an airy sigh of full content and quiet), the scarecrow's bragging hullabaloo, the Trent below, which in this mood seems gladder to be bright than strong; the trees' rustle as they feel their leaves—everything is as sweet and peaceful and monotonous as a cuckoo's chime. Could you not be content to sit here half a day and feel these influences ? "

But Polly is thinking of something else, and does not answer this rhapsody, saying decidedly, as she rises—

" I must indeed go now."

Humphrey rises with her, and picks up her bundle from the ground.

" How heavy it is ! " he says, looking ruefully at her. " Have you carried this all the way from Adams ? " Then with a sudden shamefaced effort : " Let me carry it a little way."

" No, no, Mr. Humphrey."

" Only to the gate."

" I cannot think of it, sir. Please to give it me back, or I will not stir."

While they are so disputing, a gentleman with two ladies appear in the avenue that makes the principal approach to the church. They are at once so interested in the matter, that their acquaintance with one at least of the parties is evident. Would you know their names ? That tall, pale, well-dressed young lady, fine but haughtily featured, is Miss Manlove. The lady who is giggling is Miss Flighty. Their escort, Mr. Thomas Chatterly, junior, a good-looking young man, with good clothes, a good digestion and good temper, to speak only of his good parts. Mr. Chatterly opens the gate for the ladies, and all three advance towards the disputants.

"Why, good afternoon, Denton," says Mr. Chatterly, with a waggish look at the bundle. "Glad to see you."

"Very glad to see you," echoes Miss Flighty, with smirking emphasis.

"Is it Mr. Denton?" says Miss Manlove, too calm and cold to be scornful, as she fits her eye-glasses to her nose. "Indeed it is! I am very glad indeed to see you, Mr. Denton, especially under circumstances so charming."

Denton only answers these compliments with a bow, trying to deny to himself that he is abashed.

"A very fine day, Denton," says Chatterly, flourishing his stick, and casting his eye in mock admiration on all the beauties around, including Polly.

" Yes," replied Denton.

He could not have answered more shortly unless he said " No."

Now it is Miss Manlove's turn.

" You do not introduce us to this lady, Mr. Denton ; a cruel reticence."

The young man made a great effort, mentally sentencing himself to self-command or death, and answered gravely—

" Polly Berridge, Miss Manlove. Those who cultivate her acquaintance find it most valuable."

The tormentor responded in her quiet, invariable, slightly drawing tone—

" I shall be delighted, I am sure, to become a humble member of the circle of her admirers. It is a very pretty walk this way, Miss Berridge ? "

Polly declining the opening, Chatterly takes it up.

"Under pretty conditions, eh, Denton? We shall not have your company to Nottingham, I suppose ? Well, good-day. We shall see you this evening, I hope, at Mrs. Feathers' ! "

" O, yes, we must of all things," cried Miss Flighty ; and the trio, having completed bows of wonderful length and breadth, sail away.

Polly turns to Humphrey with a glowing face and flashing eyes, and catching her bundle from him, says both reproachfully and angrily—

" You see you have made both yourself and me ridiculous ! " So leaving him.

Half-stunned, Humphrey lets her go, and stands upbraiding himself.

" I'm forsworn if my heart chopped up small with bread would make a meal for a jay. Why are my cheeks and tongue so guilty ? Have I been committing a crime ? Surely not. Or a fault ? No. A folly perhaps ? Well, I partly believe not—or if I were, woe to the fool that has not the courage of his foolery. The valiant in folly has half the merit of a wise man, but the timorous fool is twice a fool. They have gone away bursting their sides with genteelly restrained laughter; and she in as much anger as her heart knows of ; by which she looks more amiable than ever. I must go after her, and make my peace as wisely as I have wit for."

So the last of the intruders has gone, and left us free to walk round the old fabric that has now the serene beauty of antiquity, though its youth, I dare say, was but a gawky one. Enough, however, has been seen, and the twilight begins to fall. Let us return home, and on the way I will give some further account of Mr. Denton, whom we have met here to-day.

He is said to be of good birth; but all I know about that is, that his father and mother were better people than are often seen, and therefore of bad birth he cannot be. Whether or no, he lives with his mother, a widow not yet elderly, in the largest house in the village; a great, square, red-brick place, as ugly as could be built for money (as to love it is unknown in the building trade), but comfortable withal, and surrounded by fine gardens and plantations that half redeem its plainness. He is also supposed to be sole heir to his uncle, Mr. Paul Denton's property.

This was the elder brother of Humphrey's father, and a man of much experience. He has travelled; was a soldier in his young days, and when he left the army, made himself a barrister to employ his leisure. He is said to have been especially skilful in cross-examination, but has now given up practice. He possesses a good estate within a few miles of Wilford, to which village he rides round two or three times a week, paying his sister-in-law a visit longer or shorter according as his nephew is at home or not, and also calling on a few old friends in the neighbourhood. Formerly he used to dine in London with the wits ; here in the country he is well enough liked, but with something of doubt. If you would know how he looks, he is short and stout, with a keen eye, and aquiline nose, and carries himself erect.

But here we are back again, and you are weary of me, though you will not say so. Farewell for the present.

CHAPTER II.

THE cottage of the Berridges' still stands at the further end of Wilford, near the lane that leads to the Trent Bridge. It is a thatched and patched building, ranked sideways to the road on which it abuts. Mark the gray belly-ing walls, the tiny casements, and the little latticed porch facing the south. In the front is a garden, the borders of which bloom, in spite of the lateness of the season, with rose, geranium, and verbena; while the rest of the plot is green with kidney beans, cabbage, and celery. At the rear there is a large orchard, famous for its apples as far as Nottingham. Amos Berridge, the occupier, had formerly been a framework knitter at Nottingham, but having, like many of his class, a fondness for gardening, had some few years before the time that we speak of, retired hither with his small savings, and set up as market gardener, the dream of his youth. If all youthful ambi-tions were as moderate, they would oftener be realised ; and, being so, be enjoyed. He has one son, Mike, employed in a lace factory, and one daughter, Polly, who is a mender for one of the great warehouses.

In the dusk of the day on which we saw Humphrey Denton meet his daughter Polly in the churchyard, Amos stood at his cottage door smoking ; an ageing man with bent shoulders, and a gentle face that has seen troubles. While he is there his daughter comes up the garden path, a manly shape at the same time being dimly perceived to turn away from the gate.

" Is that Mr. Humphrey, lass ? " said Amos quietly, and barely looking at her, as if to say, " Don't answer me if you'd rather not, you know."

" Yes, father."

" Has he come up wi' thee ? "

" Yes, father."

" He does so often, lass ! "

" Yes, father."

" Ah," said Berridge, with something like a sigh, as he turned in.

Polly lights a candle, and while she hangs her bonnet and shawl behind the stair-door, we may take a quiet survey of the room.

C

A quaint place, indeed, showing the different work of several generations. The floor is partly of brick and partly boarded. One side of the roof slopes, until the smallest man could touch it with his head ; the other portion is flat and crossed by a rugged beam, from which hang bags of herbs. Two cushioned arm-chairs stand like sentinels on either hand of the gaping chimney, in which is a huge grate reduced to a reasonable size with bricks. The walls are well white-washed and adorned with brightly-coloured prints. Do not be too much surprised if you see in the nook between the window and the chimney a little piano. A poor jingling thing, no doubt, which your dainty fingers, young lady, would scorn to touch ; picked up cheap at an auction, but under Polly's fingers it makes music which her father, and mother, and brother, and some one else loves.

"Why, what is it, lass ?" said Berridge, as Polly brought her face to the light. " Thou looks all ill to fare. Has any one said oat to thee ?" he suddenly asked, almost fierce at the suspicion.

" O no, father."

He laid his pipe down on the table, and, putting both his hands on her shoulders, looked with fatherly confidence into her face, saying—

"What grieves thee, my lass?"

"O, father," she cried, bursting into tears, and falling on his neck, "he keeps meeting me, and he oughtn't, he oughtn't. I went round by the churchyard to-day, and he met me again."

"Ne'er mind, my lass, ne'er mind," said the father's pity, comforting her like a child, as he pressed her to him, and put his rough cheek on her smooth one. "There, there. Hang on feyther. Nay, nay."

When she had been a little soothed by his gentle admonitions, he drew her to his old arm-chair by the chimney, and set her on his knee, fondling her with rugged tenderness.

"Now art better?" he murmurs, in a soft tone for a man, and a working man, too, that had nearly done a life's work. "Art better now? Wi' thee lying on feyther's knee like a little wench, I feel like to begin wi' lullaby babby, or some other oad nonsense. Ay, many's the time I've lullabied thee to sleep wi' thy pretty face. Ah, oad times, oad times. Thou'st thy babby face yet, lass."

"Dear father," was answer enough and thanks enough, with the caress that went with it.

There they sat unspeaking with their hearts so close together, both thinking of the same thing. Polly's thoughts I could not venture to interpret, so wildly changeable they were, taking a fresh dye from every imagination, especially the somberer ones. Her father, too, was trying, without any ingenuity, to solve the question. He thought well of the young gentleman; he loved his frequent visits; and wise or otherwise, with what face could he ask him to discontinue them? He knew how to trust his daughter with his honour as well as her own; and this was his conclusion, with one prayer to leave all to Him to whom he had surrendered every tittle of his life.

Now bursts in brother Mike, a tall, big-jointed, ungainly colt, yet with a clean and bright face. He flings his hat as it happens, and then, staring with great eyes at the group in the arm-chair, cries, boyishly boisterous—

"Hullo, what's up wi' our Poll?"

"Ne'er mind, lad," answered the father; "it's nothing."

"I'm not going to be shoved o' one side," said the son, rebelliously. "I'm going to mind a jolly lot. Our Poll don't have megrims about nothing. What's matter, Poll?"

"I'll tell you another time, Mike, perhaps," the girl answered.

"All right," says the unsuspicious Mike. "I don't want to hurry; I only want to know as all's right with our Poll. But if somebody does want anything"—showing a powerful arm—"I can give it him."

"No, Mike," said Polly, rising with a smile to kiss him. "No one wants anything; every one is quite contented with nothing. Do I look all right now?"

"I should like to hear as anybody looks righter," cried Mike, half angry at his own supposition. "Now, where's my supper? You're on to clamming me; that's what it is."

"Ay," said the father, as he left the room, smiling through his trouble, "get the lad his supper; he features to be pinched very nigh."

The deft Polly soon supplied the famishing

boy, who showed the dreadful extent of his previous privations by the violence with which he now satisfied his famine. Nevertheless, after a few minutes' silent exertion, he suddenly shouted, with his mouth full, to his sister, who was three yards distant—

"I say, Polly!"

"Yes, Mike."

"Ain't it spanking?"

"Glorious!" cried Polly, seeming to understand her brother's thoughts.

"I say!" he yelled again.

"Yes."

"I wish next May was to-morrow!"

"That would be rather awkward," said Polly, "for then, you see, to-morrow would be next May. A long time to wait for breakfast, eh?" she added, skilfully appealing to his more sensitive feelings. "I'm going to make a scholar of you, Mike."

"Don't," he said, shrinking; he was too healthy to turn pale.

"It's my desire, sir," was the decided rejoinder.

"Oh, very well," said Mike, at once carelessly submissive. "I won't objeck."

Polly seized the opportunity to begin his lessons at once.

"Say object, Mike, not objeck. O, b, j, e, c, t —object."

"Object," Mike repeated, apparently without troubling himself much about the matter.

"Now shall you remember?" asked the professor.

"Well, you see, Poll," he replied, rubbing his pate, "if 'twas a bit o' machinery, or a gun, or a bat, or summat I could lay hands on—"

"I'll show it you in a book, and that will impress it on your stupid head."

"Will it?" enquired Mike, doubtfully.

"See here. What is that, sir?" she said, with severity, tweaking his ear.

"O, b, j, e, c, t—object. Ay, it's there fair an' square. But s'pose books are allus right, though?"

"Well—hm—not always," answered Polly, truthfully, but doubtful of destroying the illusion.

"Then they ain't so clever, eh, after all?" the cross-examiner pursued.

"Well, not always," again the conscientious witness replied.

Grim reality now dimly loomed on the young man through the fictitious vapours of ignorance.

" I thought they only wrote cos they'd—"

" They'd what, Mike ? "

" Like bust, if they didn't."

" Burst, Mike."

" Ah, they'd burst, would they now ? "

Just then the cottage door opened, and before anything was visible at it but a big basket, Mike screamed, at the top of his voice—

" Mother, I'm to play for the County next season. Hooray ! "

Even Polly chimed in with a sympathetic " Hooray ! " and waved her hand as Mrs. Berridge appeared ; a stout, comfortable dame, with a bright ribbon in her bonnet, and an honest red on her cheeks ; having a motherly smile in, not on, her face, and matronly sharpness on, not in, her speech.

" Well," quoth she, as she set her basket down and unloosened her bonnet-strings, " Well, I hope you're happy now you've a chance of getting yourself killed off with a cricket-ball. But if it was cannon-balls, it'd be all the same to you."

"Happy!" answered the delighted Mike; "I feel as if I could—. I wish I'd got a drum to whack at!"

"You'd better not, lad," said Mrs. Berridge, as tartly as if she heard the performance. "I know what drums are. I've been in a family, and that was Mrs. Wagner's, at Lowangrin House, where there was ten children, and a drum apiece they did have, let alone trumpets, and whistles, and rattles, and good loud voices of their own. Missis was always saying as discord was the soul of harmony; and soul enough of it we had there; besides her always nagging at the master about a man he knew called Mozart, a Jewish sort o' name, and a bad character, too, if all missis said was true, which wasn't gospel about gravies, at all events. Anyhow, they was always a mixing him up with a Bait-oven, as they said, which I never saw in the kitchen, though that Mozart might ha' stolen it. And there was a Handle, too—dear-a-me, how she did go on about it—as might be the handle to the oven. But, as I was saying, lad, there's noise enough in th' house with your shouting, and stamping, and whistling, and—"

"And Polly's singing," suggested Polly, laughing.

"Bless your face."

Mrs. Berridge had by this time, with Polly's help, taken off her trappings, and emptied her basket, and now seated herself comfortably in the arm-chair. Throwing herself back, with a sigh of content, she said—

"Who do you think came up with me from the ferry?"

"George Parr!" was Mike's conjecture.

"George Parr?" said Mrs. Berridge, shortly, "and who's George Parr?"

"Law, don't you know, mother? Best leg-hitter in the world. Why, last month, at Lord's—"

"Bother your lords, and ladies, too. It was Mr. Humphrey; if that isn't good enough. Mrs. Watson, that used to be at the Manloves', tells me he's wonderfully taken with their oldest young lady."

"I like Mr. Humphrey," said Mike, very decidedly. "Don't you, Poll?"

"No, I don't," she answered, pettishly.

Ah, Polly!

"Well, I'm sure!" the mother burst in,

indignantly; "you're hard to please, child. The nicest and pleasantest young gentleman! And so fond of your father, too! You ought to be ashamed, and—" this with a shake of the finger—"and should be, if you were two minutes younger, or I'd know the reason."

"Don't he like you, Poll?" asked the too curious Mike.

Polly was busy with her back to him at the other end of the room, but when the question was repeated, could answer—

"It's not very likely."

"Well," quoth he, pondering it deeply, "he's a rum 'un, if he don't." Then dismissing that matter as incomprehensible, he enquired again, "But now, why don't you like him, Polly?"

"Mercy on the boy and his questions!" exclaimed Mrs. Berridge.

"Why don't you, Polly?" he persisted, unabashed.

"Haven't you finished your supper?" said Polly, evasively.

"Not a bit of it. But now why—?'

"Bless the girl!" suddenly cried Mrs.

Berridge, to her relief, " she hasn't changed her boots ! "

" They're quite dry, mother ; look ! "

" I don't want to look," she answered, turning her head away ; " I should know what boots are before this. You change them, Polly, or straight you go off to bed. I've enough on my hands without having you laid up with a sore throat, and messing about all day with poultices and beef tea."

Polly being thus dismissed to make the needful change, the mother all at once bounced up, and began vigorously to remove the supper things.

" Mother, I've not done yet," Mike remonstrated.

" Then you'll have to ha' done, lad. If your belly don't ache, it's a pity but it does ! "

During this colloquy the father had returned to his habitual corner of the chimney, so that on Polly's entrance, the family circle was complete. Complete, since no member was absent ; and more truly still, because there was no flaw in their union ; no envy, no debate, no mistrust, no cankerous thought.

After they had chatted a little or been silent at will, the mother doing most of the talk, Polly took up a book and began to read aloud. Perhaps not all the listeners could have told you that she was reading the first volume of Mr. Macaulay's "History of England," recently published. What they loved was the voice; the rest did not matter much. Thus they sat getting gradually drowsier under the day's fatigue and the fire's warmth, until Amos, waking with a start from a momentary nap, said—

"Now then, Polly, for feyther's favouright. It's gone nine."

While her father filled his pipe, that he might enjoy the music the better, Polly went to the piano, and after a prelude not badly played, began that most plaintive of ditties, "Auld Robin Gray."

She was still complaining that "Auld Robin Gray came a-courting me," when a carriage was heard to stop outside. In a minute some one knocked, who, on Mike's opening the door, proved to be Mr. Humphrey. He explained that since he had to pass the cottage on his way to an evening party at Mrs. Feathers', he had taken the opportunity to bring them a book, which he thought they would like to see.

Polly received it on behalf of the family with a few subdued thanks, and, surrounded by the others, proceeded to open it.

" A famous book appearantly," said Amos, taking his pipe from his mouth; while Mike read out the title—

" The Personal History of David Copperfield."

" Dear-a-me " cried Mrs. Berridge, " and pictures too."

Interrupting their exclamations the visitor asked—for he saw the piano open—to hear a song before he left. Would Polly sing the " Bailiff's Daughter of Islington? " Not in the habit of refusing for her own pleasure, she sat down again and went through the piece with comical mock pathos. The young gentleman took his seat with the rest, while she sang, a strange contrast to the homely surroundings in his faultless evening dress. When she rose, he thanked her, and in a minute was whirling along in his brougham to how different a scene !

"Ah, it's a strange world," said Berridge. "To think o' folks sleeping half the day and partying all through the night, as if they despised God's blessed sun."

"It isn't Mr. Humphrey's fault," Polly ventured to say. "He must do as others do."

"Ay," her father answered, "and it's o' them others I'm talking, not of him. Though to my thinking if we're content allus to do as others do, it's little good we shall do; and that little waint be our own."

But it is late. Polly will hand the father his big Bible, out of which he will read a chapter with a solemn voice, full of emotion; he will offer a short broken prayer; and so good night and peace be unto this house.

CHAPTER III.

Mrs. Feathers lives at West Bridgford, a village facing the Trent bridge, from which its name, and not more than a mile and a half from Wilford. She is a happy widow with a large grown-up family, for whose benefit, as she says, she enjoys to the utmost a constant whirl of party-giving and going. Her house is large and old-fashioned, with numberless passages and rooms opening into one another; the very place for the disposal of a multiform assemblage such as is gathered there to-night. Everywhere is disorderly abundance; in one room dancing, in another cards; here conversation, there music; nay, there is even a nook sacred to man and tobacco; while happy couples wander to and fro, at their will. But none of the party, I fancy, are better amused than a little group in the hall. Their eager whisperings, malicious smiles, merry eyes, and suppressed laughter, mark them at once as engaged with some choice piece of scandal. There is Miss Teens, a boisterous romp of fifteen; Miss

Scarem, a more developed Miss Teens; Miss Dragon, who may have been a loud-voiced hoyden, too, in her day, but is now an old maid under protest, with a temper disordered by disappointment and tight-lacing. In the centre are Miss Flighty and Mr. Chatterly, already of our acquaintance.

The recital has evidently been finished, and Miss Teens is exclaiming—

" What fun!" tossing her hair in a brainless giggle.

" Can it be credited?" says Miss Dragon's thin sharp voice; without any appearance of doubt however.

" Yes, indeed," cries Miss Scarem, " or it would be the death of all amusement."

" Is it true," asks Miss Dragon again, " that he has been paying particular attention to Miss Manlove?"

Miss Dragon deals much in questions.

" Oh, I could die of laughing!" cries Miss Teens.

" Poor Sophia!" sighs the sympathetic Miss Flighty.

Just then Miss Manlove herself passed, bearing erect her usual haughty indifference.

"How pale she is!" tittered Miss Scarem.

"How flushed her cheek!" said Miss Dragon.

Then swallowing her satisfaction like an oyster in vinegar and pepper, she turned to Miss Manlove, saying—

"What a horrible occurrence, my dear."

"Which?" answered that lady, with all calmness, "I have heard of three in these five minutes."

"Oh, this revelation about Mrs. Denton's boy, my dear. You may be assured I pity—"

"Whom, Miss Dragon?" asked the other, after vainly waiting for the pity to come fairly out.

"Oh, all the parties interested, my dear."

"That seems to be yourself more than any one."

"Well," retorted Miss Dragon, "you certainly know best."

"No, Miss Dragon, I have not the assurance to compare my knowledge of anything with that of one so much older and better informed than myself."

"Well," concluded Miss Dragon, in a spasm of bitterness, "I hope that patience and resignation will be exercised under the trial."

"Surely, Miss Dragon, you will not find those virtues difficult with all the practice that you have had."

Miss Dragon stands with a cankered smile on her face, searching her heart for an answer and finding abundant malice but no wit. During the above colloquy much urgent whispering and motioning had passed between the Misses Scarem and Teens; and now the latter breaks out with a sudden clang like a tuneless bell-clapper.

"Are you really engaged to him, Miss Manlove?"

"To whom, my dear?" asked Miss Manlove, reading her all over with passionless, remorseless eyes, under which she began to feel very young indeed, but mustered imprudence to reply—

"Oh, Humphrey Denton, of course."

"You will find, child," as you grow up answered the lady, looking down on her with unresentful scorn, "that persons are not so eager for an engagement, unless they have passed or not yet reached the age of its probability. Children and elderly ladies who have not the opportunity of making attachments, are fond of imagining them."

With that she swept away, bowing at the same time to a gentleman at the door who was entering, and turned out to be Humphrey Denton himself.

He would fain have passed the tattle-mongers without notice, but was forestalled by Miss Scarem, who started at once to meet him, followed by Miss Teens.

"Let me congratulate Mr. Denton," she said, all smiles.

"I must be fortunate," he answered, forcing himself to make a mask of his face, "without my knowledge."

"Oh, you know, you wicked creature," she said, almost seeming to admire his wickedness.

"Believe me," he replied, "you praise me for more wickedness, and depreciate me for more knowledge than I am aware of."

"The lady of the bundle! Oh, you know!"

"Hm—ah—yes," said Humphrey, at intervals, striving to recollect, and at last manifestly succeeding.

"What's her name?" giggled out Miss Teens.

"Pardon me, Miss Teens; you have doubtless so great a superiority of knowledge on most points of the subject, that you must allow me to retain that trifling advantage."

Miss Teens, not well understanding with her dull wits, was a little reduced if not abashed, and left it to Miss Scarem, who proceeded—

"She's not a gipsy, is she? Is she so very savage?"

"Had she received your breeding and education, Miss Scarem, she would doubtless have been very different. But we always make allowances for a lady, even when they are needed."

"Indeed!" she replied, with an indifferent effort to appear indifferent; "I thought you were so hard to please?"

"A huge mistake; some amuse me without effort, without even the labour of an intention."

They had now reached the foot of the stairs, on which Chatterly and Miss Flighty, were sitting. Both rose, the former saying with a nod, " How do, Denton ?   But I have seen you before to-day."

" Have you seen me twice, Chatterly ? Then you may be said to have seen double for once."

Mr. Chatterly was inclined to indulge in cups, and Mr. Chatterly sat down again.

" I believe I, too, have seen Mr. Denton before," said Miss Flighty, with smiling blandishments.

" A pleasure, Miss Flighty," answered Humphrey gallantly, " to meet you any-where."

" A pleasure, Mr. Denton, to meet you there.   You looked delightfully ridiculous."

" If a pleasure is according to its rarity, that must be the most delightful of all.   A dish more epicurean than nightingales' tongues, an aloe blossoming in a hundred years, the white elephant of delights, the phœnix of amusements, encountered more seldom than anything that is ever met."

Very poor fun all this, no doubt; coarse-ness for sarcasm, effrontery for wit, malice for everything ; lungs without head, and belly without heart.   Alas ! my friends, that was thirty years ago, and we are better than our fathers. We have been to school with many doctors, and have learnt, even in the country, to wound gently, torture artistically, ruin politely.

While the disconcerted and puzzled tormentors, like gadflies dispersed by angry umbrellas or handkerchiefs, are hovering aloof, uncertain whether to collect for another onslaught, or seek a tamer prey, they are checked and dispersed by the entrance of Mr. Paul Denton. A man feared by some dull people, who, when there was a laugh, did not know whether the joke was not against themselves. The uncle and nephew, being alone, looked at one another for a minute, the one keenly, the other unquailing. Then the former, reckoning up Humphrey's excited eye and unusual flush, began gravely, shaking his head—

"You have drunk too much wine, Humphrey."

"I have but just entered," he answered, turning himself impatiently. "But no need of wine as long as these rampant fools live to claw one's spirits."

"You had better go," said his uncle, touching him on the arm; "you will expose yourself.   Drinking, and other things—you understand me, I have heard something—are not thought well of now in public; they are of *mauvais ton*, and none but blackguards are seen to do them.   In my earlier days it was proper to be improper; but now that is changed, and we're all virtuous *à la mode*. For while we are in the world, we must do as it does; we must do as society, if we would be of it.   If it prays, I pray, there is no help; if it swears, I swear, and willingly. Don't be strait-laced, my boy; doctors concur that it damages the constitution; but what fashion puts in penalty avoid, eschew, abhor. That is the deadly sin, when it is seen; like some of our queer friends whom we must cut in public, but in private—as you please."

Ah, if Mr. Denton were given the grace perfectly to follow his religion!   But he has backslidings—yes, many backslidings.   Anyhow, his further admonitions were interrupted by the approach of a lady, mature and matronly, but by no means faded, clothed in something dark.   Everything, even her eyes, was at rest; her dress lay quietly graceful around her, rustling as softly as her thoughts might do. Mrs. Denton was not a woman to single out of a crowd, yet very noticeable in a room, most important in a life. Her hair was bound in close braids round her head.

Mr. Paul Denton rarely stayed long in his sister-in-law's company; not from disrespect, for he admired her; nor from dislike, for he had even some affection for her, and more-over honoured her as the representative of a brother whom he had loved. Perhaps it was only a habit of taste that made him sup best on his usual diet. This night, after glancing into her face, where he thought he saw some-thing, he left her without a word. Humphrey took little note of anything but his thoughts.

His mother called his name, and when he had answered without turning, went nearer and spoke lower.

"What is wrong with you, Humphrey?"

"Is anything?" he answered, "or more than usual?"

Ah, I fear those goadings have roused a pride that would have lain quiet enough.

"Nay, I ask you, my son."

"Nothing is wrong," he answered again, "as far as I know, more than usual, with me."

"Are you quite sure of it, Humphrey?"

She spoke with a touch of calm, patient, sorrowful questioning in her voice.

"No," he replied, with young self-will refusing the confidence that he knew would be so sweet.

"What then?" enquired the mother's solicitude, which also had its own bounds and fences, restraining by the name of trespass from fields where it longed to wander at ease. "What then?"

"I am moderately sure, mother, reasonably sure. Is not that enough?"

Nothing is so contagious as heat and cold. The sun's least increase in the torrid zone will affect the shivering poles, and a whiff of new cold in the arctic regions moves all things, even to the equator.

"You must determine, son," she answered with more dignity, if equal love and patience. "It is neither my duty nor pleasure to be the spy on your actions, or the judge over them.

That would suit neither my inclinations nor my conscience, Humphrey. To me all is as you say; and all's very well, for so do you say."

The mother took her son's arm, and both passed again among the company to enjoy the evening as they could; Mrs. Denton as placid as ever, Humphrey more gay than usual. Would it be a happier world or no, if we all carried our thoughts plainly on our faces? There would be much more un-happiness visible. But again, many of the feebler sorts of misery, brought to the open air from the cellars and hot-houses where they flourish rankly, would take cold and die. Doubtless he is the happiest soul who shows most of himself. Even in the trashiest plays it is the gloomier dummies that soliloquise and wrench their wigs in solitude.

CHAPTER IV.

Two or three days after this Mr. Paul Denton was sitting in his sister-in-law's morning-room, engaged, I suppose, in thinking, like most persons who are doing nothing else. Mrs. Denton was altogether busied with some sort of needlework. Ladies have that happy resort from care. I dare say they sat so half an hour without a word, until Mr. Denton said at last, with the extreme carelessness of premeditation—" Where is Humphrey, Martha ? "

" I do not know," she replied, being too much occupied at that moment with her work for a longer answer.

Stout-hearted, keen Paul Denton was almost afraid of that calm sister of his, and paused before he said again, " You and he are a little out, I see."

But Mrs. Denton did not hear or understand.

" I beg your pardon, Paul ? "

Mr. Denton was obliged to speak more plainly.

"You are not on very good terms with Humphrey just now, I fear."

"You are mistaken, Paul."

"By you then, Martha," he retorted, gaining courage as he heard his tongue wag, "you and he are at present like two useful pleasant salts that unite into a freezing mixture. You send me from your joint presence aching with cold. If this continues you must double your fires."

"I do not know from what you infer this,' said Mrs. Denton.

"From my feelings," he answered. "When I feel cold, I infer that I am cold. Come, be candid with me; you have heard this something about Berridge's girl."

"Excuse me, Paul; Humphrey has given me no information of any such matter."

"Of course not," replied the man of the world; "that would be too liberal, even for a libertine, which he by no means is. You have made shift to borrow the information elsewhere."

"No, Paul, I have not, and I will not. I can trust my son, or ought. At any rate, I am not willing to have any distrust of him;

and I will know no more of him than he chooses.   Shall you dine with us to-day?"

"Yes, yes," he answered.   "And for all this talk of trust, you distrust him so much that you shut your eyes, fearing to see."

Mrs. Denton only shook her head, for she disliked controversy, conscious that in it a glib tongue has too great an advantage.

"Come, what shall we do with him, the scapegrace?"

No answer.

"When a doctor cannot relieve his patient he bids him travel, and gets rid of him.   Let us follow the rule in Humphrey's case.   A few months on the Continent will work more cure than gallons of rebuke, bushels of advice, and all the pills of wisdom ever boxed in the wisest head."

But Mrs. Denton was engaged with a little knot in her thread, and did not answer.

"Is not that your opinion?"

"If Humphrey please," she answered simply, still busy as before.

"No, no," he said, a little irritated by her calm refusals; and to know how irritating calmness may be, you need not have been be-

calmed for a week at the equator. " No, no ;
if Humphrey does not please, and the more
needful the less he pleases. If our patient
is eager for the journey, home air will suffice.
If he takes the parting like a pill, it may act
as one, and cure him; if he takes it for a
sweet it will only clog his digestion. It might
be well, besides, to give Berridge a hint; it
could not harm, done prudently. If you think
proper, I—"

" Paul, if you have anything to say about
Humphrey, I must not hear it. To my mind
it would be treachery towards him to take
any knowledge of him from another. Stay"—
for she saw her brother-in-law's mouth open
full of reasons—" whatever it be, wise or
otherwise, still I will not do it."

" Well, well, Martha, when he was little I
suppose you never washed him till he confessed himself dirty ? "

" He is not little now."

" And yet no Nestor."

" I will not argue with you, Paul; " this
in the quiet tone that makes ratiocination
quake in his shoes more than thunder. " No
argument that makes right wrong or

the mean noble can be just, however specious."

"That is to say," quoth he, "my arguments are false, because they prove my case."

"Yes, Paul, I know they are false, because they prove falsehood."

And, looked at rightly, is there a better test in the world for an argument than what it proves?

Into what depths of logic Mr. Denton would now have dragged and drowned us cannot be known, for he was prevented by the appearance of Humphrey at the door. He looked in, and his next impulse seemed to be to look out again. However, he advanced with great resolution and greeted his uncle.

"Humphrey," said the latter, opening at once, "have you heard lately of young Trainer?"

"Not since he reached Naples," replied the nephew.

"And how does he like Italy?"

"O, he likes the parties freely, and is obliged to like the ruins. He'll return, I suppose, with a wife, a few battered Brumma-gem statuettes, and the right to screw up his left eye in a picture gallery."

"Why should not you follow our Jason's example, and sail back in your Argo with Medea and the spoils of many countries?"

"And well fleeced?"

Mrs. Denton now found it necessary to gather up her work and leave the room, just as the uncle was saying—

"Seriously, you should marry, Humphrey."

"I intend to marry, seriously, uncle. But why, if I may ask, have you not followed your own precept?"

"I had a disappointment in my youth," he replied.

"I beg your pardon," said Humphrey, in some confusion; "I had not heard of that."

"Yes, the young lady to whom I proposed accepted me, at which I turned tail in a fright."

Thus will a counsellor destroy his own advice, for it is hard to be both witty and wise at once.

Perhaps, however, we wrong Mr. Denton;

E

he may have had somewhere an old, deep sore that he durst only touch lightly. But Mr. Gray is announced, and an elderly gentleman enters the room ; to whom Mr. Denton, without any other salutation, cries—

" Mount, mount thy grey, my gallant Gray, and charge ! "

" Where lies the enemy, most doughty Denton?" the new-comer promptly returned.

" Here," answered Mr. Denton, pointing to Humphrey.

" They seem in small force."

" But strongly posted behind good intentions; and therefore I bid you charge, charge them to marry."

" Ha ! " said Mr. Gray ; " is that the battle ? "

" Look," said the uncle, " here is a young fellow of the age, spirit, opportunity and means to marry, if he would only mean to marry."

" Certainly," said Mr. Gray sententiously, " a desirable marriage is to be desired, and a good wife is no bad thing."

" O, the stout charge! O, the brave thrust ! Fight on, my Gray ! Victory is certain *sans* my aid. I will not diminish your glory by sharing it. I leave both him and it to you."

So saying, Mr. Denton left the two companions together; for such they were, in spite of the disparity in years.

But you must grant me space to introduce Mr. Gray to you with unusual respect.

He is a man of about fifty years, tall and thin, with a doubtful, slight stoop. No, he is upright now; it was merely a tall man's knack. His face is pale, handsome, sensitive, and intelligent, and bears short whiskers, greyish and well-trimmed. Without doubt Mr. Gray was a dandy in his youth, and is handsomely and exactly dressed now, though in the fashion of twenty years ago. He carries a gold-headed cane in his well-gloved hand. He has been acquainted with Mrs. Denton from infancy, and on her marriage took rank with the Dentons as one of their most intimate friends. But with none did he exchange so much sympathy as with Humphrey, whose inmost confidences he has shared since the former was of age to have a secret; that is, since he was old enough to keep an apple to himself. In short, there was much well-balanced familiarity between them that never toppled over the bounds of due respect.

Humphrey now drew up to his elderly comrade and said—

"I have been wishing to see you, Mr. Gray; I want your advice."

Said Mr. Gray, with something like a laugh—

"O, that's your commonest want; but do you want to follow my advice?"

"Of course," answered Humphrey, sincerely resolute.

"Then you are in bad straits, Humphrey, between my advice and your wants."

"You hear that my uncle wishes me to marry. But how? is the question. There are so many ways in which a man may be cheated with a wife. Am I to marry a plain girl with an uglier temper for her fair fortune, like Benson? or pick up a fallen actress, like Jack Tidmas? or buy a beauty to hate me, like Richmond? Or to take another example, I have a friend," he said, changing his fluency for embarrassment, which was not lost on his acute observer; "this friend has a liking—I might say more than a liking—for—a girl."

"Good," said Mr. Gray, to encourage his hesitation.

"The daughter of very worthy people."

"Better," said Mr. Gray again.

"Of the working class."

"Ah!" said Mr. Gray, in an uncertain tone, as one that would not be astonished till the right time. "Ah!" said Mr. Gray, and said no more.

After an interval, Humphrey enquired—

"Suppose that happened to me, how should you advise me to act? Nay, never mind me —what do you say to him?"

Mr. Gray answered very deliberately—

"My opinion, if your friend will let me prose on such a theme, would be determined by some such considerations as these: In the first place—but your friend is already married, perhaps?"

On the denial,—

"Thank heaven," he muttered to himself; "it might have been. Well, in the first place, is he irrecoverably attached?"

"I think—I believe so," answered the young man, burning to say more.

"Because, if he is not—"

"There is no room for such a supposition," burst in Humphrey, too eagerly.

"If he were not, then," began Mr. Gray, marking emphasis with his hand on the chair arm, "if he were not, he might consider this, that there is no close and even junction but of equalities; unmatched surfaces leave unsightly gaps between their union."

"Sir," said Humphrey, "be sure there is no inequality of station between them that her endowments do not level."

"Ah, you have no experience of the common effects of such a marriage. Relations alienated, friends disgusted, and a constant laughing-stock kept in the house like a Court fool."

"I can imagine what I have never witnessed," answered Humphrey; "but that does not shake me, and would not disturb you if you knew her as well as I."

"I conclude," continued the older gentleman, dubiously feeling his way, "that the lady 'is such as a sensible man, like your friend, would choose for a wife ? "

"I have seen her," replied Humphrey, "and think I may say yes; with all my heart, yes."

Whereupon he gave vent to a laudation of Polly, with which these our narrow bounds dare not risk being overflowed. In short, she was pure goodness with a beautiful face. At which conclusion he paused out of breath, and careless from excitement of further concealment.

The elderly counsellor needed small part of his experience to see that in such a case there was no need of doctors, for doctors were no use. Resignedly he crossed his legs, saying —

" We will assume, then, that she is—"

" Herself," interposed the lover.

" And, being herself," pursued the interlocutor, unruffled and argumentative, " being herself, she is—"

" Like no one else."

" Well, since she is, doubtless, so worthy of love, and, doubtless, she is ready to return love"—

"There is some doubt there—at least, no certainty. My friend has restrained himself, and kept his passion yet unsuspected."

"Well, supposing that it is so?"

"Then," said Humphrey, "there is another doubt. My friend—but let me show myself as earnest as I am. I am my friend, sir, though but a very sorry one."

"Ah," answered Mr. Gray, gravely, but with no visible astonishment, "I hope you will indeed prove to be your best friend, Humphrey. But what is this other doubt of yours?"

"My mother."

"Is she aware of it, then? Does she not approve?" asked Mr. Gray, more eagerly.

"I don't know what she knows," answered the young man; "I believe it is little; and she is too scrupulous, too fastidious, too self-restrained—I scarcely know what to call it—too proud to ask."

"And you too proud, Humphrey, to answer her unasked?"

"No, sir—not proud," answered Humphrey warmly; "but suspicious to suspicion."

"What," said Mr. Gray, "half-a-dozen *aliases* for your mother's pride, and only one for your own? Is that because it needs less cover, or finds less?"

"Listen, sir. She came to me asking what was wrong with me. I answered, and truly: 'Nothing to my knowledge.' She replied: 'I want no more.' And what more could I say then?"

"Only this, Humphrey," said Mr. Gray, with something of stern sadness, "whatever was in your heart to say. By her motherhood she was entitled to that; could not sue for it, because it was her due; would not demand it, because her son withheld it."

"Yet so renouncing," said Humphrey, "claims the more for the renunciation."

"And rightly, too. Justice only asks for justice; but trust, generosity, love, cry for great returns. Nothing is so exacting as what is least exacting—nothing is so importunate as unselfishness."

"But what can I do now?" asked Humphrey ruefully. "The subject has become tabooed by mutual avoidance, constant reflection, until there is almost a superstitious

silence on it. More than once I have been
about to break into the circle, but have been
met with a look so irresponsive, that I have
stopped short and finished anyhow."

"Ah! you've rashly let the breach widen
into a great gap, and now would faintly stop
it with sawdust and loose trash. But, my
dear boy, you don't want long sermons from
me—your own heart will preach far more
effectually if you will listen to it. I only ask
you one thing—shall you marry without your
mother's consent?"

"Having such a mother, never," answered
Humphrey. "Besides, I cannot, for under
my father's will, as you know, all my main-
tenance comes from her."

"Just so," said Mr. Gray, looking keenly at
him from under his grey eye-brows; "you
fear that she might cut your allowance off."

"Sir, I fear that she might double it, treble
it, quadruple it, and still keep her confidence
from me; overwhelm my life with every
benefit excepting her favour. I do fear
that."

"Keep that fear, my dear boy," replied Mr.
Gray, regarding him with kind, glistening

eyes, "and you will keep a better treasure than any bolder spirit. I can say no more at present; I must first consider properly what I can do and what I ought to do."

Nothing more was said on the subject. The two friends strolled out together arm in arm, each happy to talk of what pleased the other.

To me it is a very touching thing—a seemingly unequal alliance of this kind—to see the patience with which the older spirit bears his comrade's boyish waywardness, the equanimity with which he administers unregarded counsel, and is interested in long-discarded amusements. A brave sight, too, it is, when a young man lends his arm and conforms his step to age, listening attentively to what is, perhaps, but old-fogeyish talk, tempering his fearless familiarity with an easy respect, like a gamesome well-tempered colt that kicks up his heels from high spirits, not to throw his rider.

But Mr. Gray is still vigorous; and may he live long before he has to take odds from any companion.

CHAPTER V.

In the afternoon of the same day Berridge sat alone in his cottage engaged in preparing fruit for to-morrow's market, while his wife was at the back of the house washing, and Polly at Nottingham. Through the open window the spirits of the flowers come floating in from the garden on the tender autumn breeze. No need to look out at them; their presence is everywhere to be felt. Let us sit for a minute as that old workingman does, and shut our eyes, and see, if we can, the things that he sees. What can he know of but hard toil, short rest, coarse pleasures? How does the blossoms' scent touch him? What is the birds' quieter autumnal song to him? Has the wind, too, anything to say to him? Think of it for a minute, kind reader, while, in imagination, you draw in the fragrant air and rejoice with the late sun's glancing beams and the drowsy bees' final hum. Think of it; it will serve you a good turn, if your life is not too easy. Or if it be, it is only one yawn the more as you put down the book, and another as you take it up again.

After a while Berridge rises, for he hears a step on the gravel, and looking out whom should he see but Mr. Paul Denton. He goes to the door and is saluted by that gentleman with an affable—

" How d'ye do?"

" Why, Mr. Denton, is that you, sir? Please to walk in."

Mr. Denton does so, and takes the offered chair, saying—

" I thought as I was passing, Berridge, I would just look in on you for half a minute."

" Thank ye kindly, sir; I'm honoured to see you."

Mr. Denton looks round as he settles himself easily in the most comfortable chair, and sees a cricket-bat standing in the corner. Pointing to it, he says—

" Do you ever handle a bat now?"

" Odd times, sir, may be, for a bit o' make-believe; p'raps when Mr. Humphrey comes down."

" He is here pretty often, I suppose?"

" Yes, sir, a goodish bit. You see about ever sin' he cut his fust tooth—"

" I know, I know," said Mr. Denton, " but since he cut his wisdom tooth, or ought to have done ? "

" Well, sir," answered Berridge, too self-consciously verbose, " he's been o' th' habit o' coming down o' nights, an' gossiping a bit about cricket an' the news ; or p'raps reading a little to uz. For you know, sir, I taught him to play at cricket when he was a little 'un this height; an' many's the time—"

" Yes, yes, I know," said Mr. Denton, adding in a cautiously, careless way, " but if I were you, Berridge, I would not encourage his visits."

" How's that sir ? " said Berridge, knowing nothing, but feeling an innocent guiltiness.

In an altered voice as if he had changed the subject, Mr. Denton said—

" How does Polly get on ? I have not seen her lately."

" Rarely, sir, rarely."

" I suppose she is generally at home in the evening ? "

" Yes, sir, unless she has business away."

" Well, Berridge, you must keep Mr. Humphrey away."

" Sir," answered Berridge, " t'aint for me to do that. I could scarce harden myself to it if I saw good reason ; and that I don't."

" There are plenty of good reasons to be seen if you will only open your eyes. You understand I don't say there's anything wrong yet ; I only speak of possibilities. You have two good reasons at least ; a pretty daughter and a young visitor."

" If you mean that, sir, I'm not afraid o' my daughter ; no, nor yet o' Mr. Humphrey."

" Then you should be, Berridge. Salutary fear is our one compensation for loss of youth ; the exchange of a vintage of sparkling wines, full of pleasure and headache, for a cup of wholesome, bitter herb-tea. Mind, I don't say one word against your daughter."

" Thankye, sir," answered the working-man, a little proud, and setting himself more erect, " thankye, you've no cause."

" Except that she is very pretty."

" It's your belief, sir," said Berridge

slowly and reluctantly, "that Mr. Humphrey's—that he's no friend to uz ?"

"Nay, I do not say that; I do not know. I only speak of what we may reasonably expect from their intercourse. The least evil will be scandal, which is as injurious to reputation as the fact."

"For all that, I can't see my way. There's so many crossings; I can't see my way."

"I tell you, Berridge," said Mr. Denton, wondering how to manage that strange, thick-headed man, "I tell you their names are already in people's mouths."

Berridge rose, and raised a once powerful arm, and said huskily—

"Has any one dared to say—if he has — the Lord help me to forgive him." And he fell back on his seat with a groan.

"It is what I have heard, not what I have seen, that brings me here. However false it be, slander is as light and intractable as the wind; nay, the falser the lighter and the liker wind; truth is a weight to its buoyancy. I have seen lies welcomed that would have found no footing had they been true. Our educated palates prefer French dishes to a simpler diet, and our humoured and pampered ears find their pleasure in made tattle, spiced like a curry and served hot. Introduced as a truth, we shut our eyes on its nakedness and vote it gross; told for a calumny, it is admitted, laughed at, repeated, and in the end believed. So that for our purpose it does not matter whether the report be true or false."

"Not matter, sir?" cried Berridge. "Not matter whether base things ha' been thought and done, or a pack of oad women ha' been out to tea? Not matter whether a young man's heart's gone clean rotten so that it stinks aloud, or some folks—more's the pity —have over little to do? Not matter, sir, whether your nephew's arned names I've no heart to give him, or there's only a lie or two more i' th' world? Not matter whether my daughter—? Sir, it mayn't matter to you; it matters to me, and that vastly!"

The old man, broken with emotion, could say no more, so that there was a chance for Mr. Denton to reply with his usual placidity.

"You take me crossways, Berridge. I have an interest, too, in the matter, though I do not desire perfection in my nephew; for I do not expect it, for I have never seen it—not even in vice. Or, at least, you will allow that I wish for no scandal in the family."

" Ay," said Berridge bitterly, "above all things let's have no scandal. Let him wash his face, and let him draw him on his gloves, and be as mucky as he will under his shirt."

" Well, if we can agree to separate these young people we will not quarrel about the rest. It was my part to inform you, it is yours to take measures; and if you have any wisdom it will be a losing parsimony not to use it now."

At this point the dialogue was broken off by a knock at the door, and on Berridge's opening Mr. Denton was surprised to distinguish Mr. Gray's voice outside enquiring after the house of a person named Berridge. Being duly informed, he asked again : "Have you not apples for sale?" Amos assented, and invited him to walk in. He did so, and found himself confronting one whom he would sooner have met anywhere else.

" What ! " he said, " are you come after pippins, too, Denton?"

"No," replied the other, "nor cheese either."

Mr. Denton was, by nature, a suspicious man ; and, at any rate, was not to be sauced and eaten with apple like a ridiculous goose. He pondered what this new arrival might mean, while Mr. Gray opened his pretended business in decisive business-like style.

"Well, Mr. Berridge, I shall not take any great quantity of your apples at first ; I shall wish to give them a trial. How much are they a—a hogshead ? "

Amos was unacquainted with that new measure for apples, which perhaps obtained down south—a vague region where strange things abounded. He said—

"Do you mean a bushel, sir ? "

Mr. Gray accepted the suggestion, and was informed that the best quality was so much.

"Well, you may send me—yes, I think a quarter will be enough for the present."

"Thank you, sir," said Berridge. "You are in the wholesale line, I suppose ? "

"Not at all. This is my address."

Meanwhile Mr. Denton was laughing in-

wardly, and half ready to suspect that Polly
had something to do with the visit. Could it
be that another young woman had made
another old fool? So while Berridge was
laboriously booking the order, he took
occasion to say waggishly—

" Are you about to marry, Gray ? "

" Upon my word, Denton ! what makes you
say so ? " replied Mr. Gray, with more irrita-
tion than seemed requisite.

Duly noting this, his friend replied—

" Oh, your increased scale of housekeeping.
You find life ill-tasting, and are going to eat
it with much apple-sauce."

" The geese," said the other, " will not be
far to seek."

"Not if you find a wife, or a wife finds you."

But there is another tap at the door; again
Berridge opens it, and another voice, not unknown, is heard saying—

" I am looking for the house of a market-
gardener named Burbage or Burgage, about
here."

" P'raps you mean Berridge, sir," said the
old man; " my name's Berridge."

" Have you any golden pippins to sell ? "

"Yes, sir, if you'll come in."

The feet were heard on the step, as the voice proceeded—

"Do you ever let any of your rooms to visitors, Berridge, in the summer or autumn? I'm thinking of— Upon my word, Mr. Gray and Mr. Denton!"

"Who hopes, Chatterly," said the latter, "that on the same valuable security you are quite well."

As they were shaking hands, he had time to think—

"A pound to a penny both after the same fruit;" and then said aloud—"So you, too, are come west to gather apples, and find the Hesperides not at home?"

"What are they?" asked Chatterly, who had gone to college seriously to study cricket and boating.

"The guardians of the apples," answered Mr. Denton.

"Wasps?"

"Something, at least, with a sting."

"Then I hope they won't trouble themselves to hurry back for me, if it's at all inconvenient."

Berridge is wondering what this means, and no one seems at ease but the astute man of the world.   But before another word was said the door-latch was again lifted, and Humphrey entered, like an old friend, without knocking.

Lo! he finds himself standing in the middle of the room, surrounded by friends who would have been dearer a hundred miles away, and has to submit to their crafty eyes with much discomposure.

At last, recovering himself with a gasp, he turned to Chatterly, who stood nearest, and said bluntly—

" What are you doing here ? "

" Buying apples," replied the unabashed Chatterly, with a furtive wink. " Is that your business ?   Fine golden pippins."

He turned from Chatterly with a look of suspicious, angry scorn, and fronted Mr. Denton.

" You, uncle ? "

" To anticipate your question, Humphrey," answered that gentleman, in words underlayed with quiet sternness, " I am not buying apples.   I only visit the garden of the Hesperides to look on."

Humphrey fell back to Berridge, who was then by the window looking out and away, and whispered in his ear—

" Is anything the matter, Berridge ? "

" May be," he answered back, without turning.

But Chatterly, who could not long be quiet, now comes up to the master of the cottage, and begins talking about his apples in a loud, gay tone, as if all that could be said was a joke.

Under cover of this, Humphrey got round to Mr. Gray, who had taken the farthest corner, and enquired of him the meaning of the gathering.

" Perhaps flies and honey," was his reply ; and it was evident that he would say no more.   Should he try his uncle again ?

" Is this an appointed meeting, uncle ? "

" No ; a disappointed," he replied.

" What brings that fellow here ? " the nephew soon asked again, in huge disgust.

" I cannot say.   What brings you ? "

" Not what brings him."

" Dare you rashly affirm that ? " said Mr. Denton, fixing him with his keen eyes.

"And swear it," replied Humphrey, in a fervid whisper.

All is not ended, for now Polly shows herself at the door; but, seeing the assemblage, will come no further.

Mr. Denton, to encourage her, calls with condescending familiarity —

"How do you do, Polly?"

"I am quite well, thank you, sir," replied Polly, very correctly, but drawing back a little further.

"Won't you come in," he said, "and talk to us gallants?"

Polly began to decline, but was stopped by her father, who said—

"Come in, lass, if Mr. Denton's oat to say to thee."

Polly entered, with the colour of deep shame on her face, as those wear it who need not be ashamed. Mr. Gray rose and courteously offered his chair, which she would not accept. Humphrey drew aside, hoping that his face did not testify of his heart's emotion. Chatterly stood boldly in the middle of the room, ready with admiration, one hand on his whiskers, the other on his hip. Berridge looked on anxiously from the window, while Mr. Denton addressed her in the jocular style proper to a girl so much one's inferior.

"The fine weather, I see, has been favourable to your roses."

"Yes, sir," answered Polly, glancing out of the window and wishing herself among them; "they are looking well for the time of year."

"Two especially," said Mr. Denton, looking at her critically, as if she were framed and hung in a picture gallery.

"You mean the two white Empresses by the crimson dahlias?"

"No; I speak of two red ones much nearer to us."

But Polly still chose to be dull.

"The moss roses?"

"You have no sweetheart, Polly, it is clear; you are so slow at a compliment. If you had one, you would have taken it as soon as offered; if you had two, you would have heard it before it was spoken; three, you would have understood it before it was thought, and believed it though the whole world swore it false."

"You mean, sir," said Polly, now verily of the rose's hue, "that three sweethearts are enough to drive a girl mad."

"Ah!" answered Mr. Denton, raising his eyebrows too knowingly, "you have a preference for one?"

One could almost have thought that he glanced round at Humphrey; but if so, it was done in a twinkling.

"I do prefer one to three," said Polly, becoming chafed.

"Which one, Polly?" cried Chatterly insinuatingly. Whereupon Humphrey savagely scowling, muttered—

"Ass!"

Mr. Denton noted Polly's growing anger, and perhaps took a little pleasure in quietly baiting it.

"So you prefer one to three," he said; "and a particular private one to every general one, eh?"

"Certainly," she answered, "I prefer a private person to a general."

"So do I, Polly," cried Chatterly.

"Ass!" grumbled Humphrey; "cease your heehaw."

"Fortunate private person!" said Mr. Denton.

"Why so, sir?" asked Polly. "Most persons are not generals."

"Well said, Polly!" cried Chatterly, followed close by Humphrey's muttered— "Ass! I wish you had some hay to keep you quiet."

"Not," said Mr. Denton, "because he is private, but because you have a private preference for him."

"Then he is only fortunate with a loss of harm, if it is only because my preference is private."

"Bravo, Polly!" cried Chatterly, clapping his hands. "You're hit, Mr. Denton."

Humphrey could only bite his lip fiercely, and again mutter, "Ass!"

"You are too subtle for me, Polly," said Mr. Denton. "When did you give up lace-mending for wire-drawing?"

"I thought that wire-drawing required materials."

"And I supply none? That is, you think there is no meaning in my words."

"I hope not," she replied.

"Mind, lass," said her father gravely from the window.

"Why so?" asked Mr. Denton; but her father's voice had called her to herself, and she would not reply. "Come, why do you hope?"

It was too bad to tease her, however good-humouredly, with such questions, surrounded as she was by so many eyes. "Won't you tell me?" No, her lips were firmly shut. "Well, I'll be satisfied, if you will name this happy private person whom you prefer."

"Ay, tell us that, Polly," cried Chatterly.

"Ass!" growled Humphrey. "Where is your driver? Would no one take you at six-pence an hour?"

"Tinker, tailor, soldier, sailor?—what is he, Polly?"

There were unwonted motions in the girl's blood, and angry tears in her eyes, not roused I deem by the words so much as the presence in which they were uttered; and she was ready to plunge in, when he asked again—

"Come, what do you say?"

"That if you were not an old gentleman, you would be very impertinent."

"Oho," he said, taken somewhat aback; but Chatterly cried—

"Good again! Go it, Polly!"

"Ass!" muttered Humphrey.

"Steady, lass," said Berridge; "thou'st said enough. See if mother's i' th' garden."

"She isn't, father."

"Mayhap she's upstairs."

"No, she is not. Mr. Denton may have something more to say to me."

"Yes," said Chatterly again, "settle him, Polly, while he's down."

And again Humphrey muttered, "Ass!"

"No, Polly," said Mr. Denton, "I confess myself routed. Nothing remains for me but to bury my slain, pack up my baggage, and retreat with as victorious a face as I can invent. Are you going my way, Chatterly?"

"Yes," said Chatterly. "I'll call again about the apples, Berridge. I want them for an old aunt of mine in London, to sweeten her opinion of me. Good-bye, Polly."

When they were clear off, Mr. Gray also rose, and after asking Humphrey for his company, bade Berridge good-day. The young man followed him in no amiable mood; and whispered to Polly as he passed—

"You've had plenty of callers to-day, you and the apples."

All the visitors departed, Amos began mildly to rebuke his daughter, or rather invited her to rebuke herself.

"Wasn't thee to blame, lass, speaking so to Mr. Denton?"

"I know I was, father," she replied, cooling rapidly, "but why did he tease me so before so many? He is too old for foolishness, and too young for dotage."

"You don't know as he meant anything, lass."

"Then he shouldn't have looked so meaning. Why did he come at all?"

"To rest a bit and have a little talk." But what better time to tell her what she must know? "Mr. Humphrey—he spoke about him."

"While he was here himself?" said Polly, vaguely disquieted.

"Nay, not that; before he came."

She went to the window and looked out. "See, father," she cried, "there's a bullfinch on the yew tree ! Funny rogue ! But what did he say ? "

Berridge felt like an executioner fresh to the trade, as he said : " He was talking a good while about this and that. Sad things go on, lass, with every turn o' night and day, dreadful things. He professes to think, his uncle does, he meant us no good in coming here, no good at all, much ill. Thou must keep from him altogether."

Stunned for a moment, Polly bravely recovered herself, and answered, plucking the words out by force—

" Then we'll think no more of him, father."

" He is a bad 'un, if it be true."

" Never mind. Let me light your pipe, father. It will do you good to have a smoke."

" Nay, lass," he answered with a sigh, " I've no heart for smoking." He went out of doors, half persuaded that Polly was little hurt.

Then she fell on her knees by her father's chair, and buried her face. Who would uncover it ?

" Oh, is he bad ? Is he bad ? Was all his

mirth villainy? All his gentleness and kindness villainy? All his goodness and nobility
villainy? Were all his words plots, his bene-
fits snares, his smiles and laughter arts?
Could he be so base and yet so winning?"

But Berridge re-entered; for less and less
sure in absence that Polly was heart-whole,
he had returned to reassure himself, and now
discovered her grief. He crossed the room,
and with too much pity for words, laid his
hand on her head, only able to say—

"May He comfort thee, my lass, who can
comfort thee."

"Oh, father," she cried, "can it be true?"

"Ah, my lass," he answered, "I can't
mind what to think. His own uncle! 'The
heart of man is deceitful above all things and
desperately wicked.' And yet it's mighty
hard to bring one's self to it; I seem to see
the lad afore me. However, it's better you
shouldn't see him, good or bad. Thou'st a
brave heart, my lass, an' this affliction waint
wreck thee. The least touch of evil, e'en a
bad thought, would be worse than all this.
May He comfort thee who is a Comforter
indeed!"

CHAPTER VI.

HUMPHREY, who felt aggrieved, though whether
by his mother, or uncle, or Chatterly, or Amos
Berridge, or Polly herself, or by those higher
destinies that dominate our purposes, he did
not discriminate, sulked for a few days and
then grew inclined to be forgiving, at any
rate until he knew that he was injured. In
this more amiable mood, therefore, down to
Berridge's he went on a pretext; for the
tatters of his indignant dignity still hanging
about him, he could not brook to acknowledge
what urged him thither, but dressed up a
mock reason, calling it a baby though it was
but a doll.

How he opened the gate and knocked at
the door, what he said when it was opened,
and what Mrs. Berridge replied, need not be
recorded here; is it not written in the
chronicles of every house? But whatever
Amos said on his entrance, there was a
difference in his manner. Of that Humphrey was certain, perhaps was prepared for

G

it; though how he perceived it, whether by eye or ear, or some other faculty, he could not tell. He sat there and talked of this and that, but the old man did not change. As kindly as usual—nay, when it was thought of, more kindly. Was it not strange? Gentle, moreover, and quiet, perhaps reproachful, perhaps remorseful, always grave, as if there were something dead in the house.

Was Polly dead? No, there was no secret in the mother's behaviour, nor yet in Mike's, when he entered. Their thoughts were as loud as their words. So he sat and cast his eyes about the room looking for something, and seeing Polly everywhere that she was not; while now and then he fetched up a few uninteresting words like a dry cough; for he only cared to say what he durst not. Pitiable company, no doubt, for the good dame and her son, who were too happy, however, to see anything amiss.

At length Berridge went out, and after spending five minutes in framing the innocent question, Humphrey managed to say—

"Where is Polly to-night, Mrs. Berridge?"

The answer was, that not being well, she had gone to stay with Aunt Mary at Ruddington, for a couple of days. "She was not seriously ill?" Oh, dear no; nothing but a cold or a little headache. Hearing which, Humphrey forgot his pretext, and shortly took his leave.

The more he thought of Polly's absence at that time, the less he liked it; whereupon he thought of it the more. Just as children stand queasily over their physic, tasting it fifty times instead of swallowing it at a gulp. He had half a mind to go over to Ruddington and see her; and, in fact, did take horse and ride through that village, but had not decided whether or not to call on her by the time that his horse had brought him home again.

In three days he called again at the cottage, in the evening, when surely she would be at home. But no, all the family was present but herself, and he durst not ask why. At length, however, Mrs. Berridge said what he had been longing all the while to hear—

"I wonder what Polly is doing upstairs all this time? She went away just as you

knocked, Mr. Humphrey.   What in the world
can she be thinking of, burning two candles
where one 'll serve, as if tallow went about
on its knees, begging you to burn it?   Call
her down, Mike."

"Nay," said Berridge, from his silent
corner, "let her be, wife, let her be.   I'll
warrant she's at no harm."

"And who said she was, Amos?" cried
Mrs. Berridge.   "I'm sure she's the best
girl in the world, and as easy to manage as a
baby, for you've only to say, and she does.
Though this I know, that she wants looking
after; for she'll sit over a book, Mr.
Humphrey, she will, till her eyes are bat-
blind, and her back as double as old Ben
Crook's.   It's quite a wonder what she does
know; name a book I can't that she hasn't
read, and very thankful she ought to be to
you, sir, for so kindly lending them."

This, and much more, was said, but Polly
did not appear before Humphrey departed.

On the day following he had no better
fortune.   Moreover, he tried to meet her as
she returned from Nottingham, to cross her
as formerly in her usual walks and occupa-

tions, but he was all out. Worst of all, she saw him at a distance, and—there was no mistake—avoided him. All this set the young man seriously to question himself.

What did it mean? Had his love been sighted, and she was not for him? But he had been so guarded, so hedged with caution, so masked and disguised, doing and saying nothing but in the ordinary way of friendship.

"It is unaccountable, unless—. That is as much as to say, it is accountable if—. And I must demand and examine the accounts."

There was one favourable opportunity of encountering her, which he had not yet tried. She was in the habit of frequenting the Wednesday evening service at some Methodist Chapel in the town; Halifax Place Chapel for certain, for there was none nearer then. He would meet her at the ferry, and there—. Well, his premeditation and foresight stopped at the ferry; the rest lay yet beyond the river. Of one thing he was resolved; he would not marry against his mother's will. But how could he pattern his love by her will?

He did as he wished. In the quiet of the

evening, when it is just light enough to perceive those whom we know best, he went
down to the ferry to catch Polly going to
town ; but instead was nearly caught himself
by Miss Manlove coming in the opposite
direction.   He managed to blunder into a
lane on the right hand ; but not in time to
escape that lady's keen eyes, as she came
leisurely up.   For Miss Manlove was never
in a hurry ; not even when it rained on
Sunday.

She was of opinion that Humphrey had
wronged her ; not very justly, perhaps, but
proof of that would only have made the
wrong greater.

"Ah," she bitterly noted to herself,
writing it on her heart with a corrosive pen,
"that was Humphrey Denton.   One can
understand his shame at meeting me.
Perhaps he is fearing that I shall follow him.
Oh, I see coming the sweet reason for his
loitering here."

In fact, from his retreat, Humphrey, with
beating heart, saw Polly come out of the
deepening shadow of the White House Inn
close by.

"Stop; come here," called Miss Manlove, as a lady should, quietly, and beckoning with her gold eye-glasses.

Polly hesitated, and then conquering herself, turned to the lady, who, with that calm, clear voice of hers that was never troubled, went on to say—

"You are the girl whom I saw with Mr. Denton in the churchyard?"

Polly's bloom deepened to an intense flush that showed even through the dusk, as, after a moment's struggle, she answered—

"I am."

"You silly creature!" said Miss Manlove, too superior either to exhibit her scorn or to conceal it. "You silly creature! Don't you know how these young men always use such girls as you? Throw you away, when they have done with you, into the street, into the gutter."

Polly's anger swelled, and her voice rose above its tremulousness, while she replied—

"No one, ma'am, can be treated so who is careful to be treated otherwise; no one can be thrown away who does not give herself up more than ever I will."

Stung with the proud air and high words of her beautiful opponent, the young lady replied—

"Of course you creatures always say that. You know that you are rather pretty, and talk very well for a girl in your position; and it is possible you may get all kinds of absurd notions into your head. But what do you think will be the end of it all?"

"I hope you will make it short, ma'am," answered Polly, with doubled wrath; to which Miss Manlove returned, as calmly as if she were catechising an infant—

"Are you trying to be insolent?"

"I am a poor girl; you couldn't insult me, tried you ever so hard."

"It would not be worth my while," answered the lady from her heights. "I am only warning you for your good; your concerns do not affect me. Mr. Denton is waiting yonder, as you are well aware, but if you were wise, you would have nothing to say to him."

So saying, Miss Manlove took herself away, and left Polly bursting with rebellious anger and shame.

"Oh, how cruel," cried her thoughts, "how cruel that calm breast! How insulting that unmoved eye! Her words burn with extreme of cold. But if Mr. Humphrey is yonder, as she says, I must begone. He may have, O, too much right to a share of her shameful words; but heaven knows I have no interest in them. Who shall claim them, then? She who made them; she who made them!"

Without delay she hastened towards the ferry, but Humphrey, quickly emerging from his hiding-place, sped after her. He calls her name; her heart starts, yet she does not answer, but unconsciously further quickens her pace. He draws up and calls again, so near that she must needs turn, and try to say with a trembling that will not be quiet—

"Is it you, Mr. Humphrey?"

"It is so long since you saw me, Polly," he answered, "that you do not know me!"

"Only six days, isn't it?" she replied, scarcely knowing what.

"I thought it more," he said, "but you have kept clearer and closer count than I. So it is only a week, Polly—you say a week?

—since you began to shun me? Your silence says yes. And why is this change? You have a reason, surely. What have I done? And why, if I have offended, am I not forgiven? Is my crime so great that it cannot be forgotten, must be sentenced prisoner for life to memory?"

"I have not accused you, sir, of anything," she replied.

"No, I am blameless, innocent to the most carping eye; and therefore—coldness, silence, removal. O, evidently I've done some great wrong, some intentional foul wrong! Yet, if I came humbly, asking for forgiveness, would it not be granted?"

"Yes, and freely," she replied, beating back her tears, "if there is need of forgiveness."

"Then be the same again, Polly," he said, offering to take her hand.

She could not reply, but her gesture and countenance were sorrowful with denial.

"Ah," he cried, "you forgive me because you must or ought, not because you would. Your forgiveness is a religious duty, not a friendly restoration; giving grace, peace, and comfort, it may be, to you; but what to me, whose need is the greatest? At least, let me know in what I have trespassed."

"I can't tell you, sir. You must question others if your own heart doesn't reveal it, or better let it rest."

Here Polly drew away, leaving Humphrey motionless with surprised grief; but ere she had gone six paces she stopped, and, half-turning, added, in a very low voice, almost as if she must say what she would not have heard—

"Unless it is false."

"Surely it is false!" cried Humphrey, starting up to her; "unless I've been mad this six days. Speak, Polly! If we find happiness together, why should we remain apart for want of a word or two, because of a word or two?"

"You must forgive us if we're unjust to you."

"I must forgive, thou must forgive, he must forgive; and still keep resentment in our hearts blocking out reconciliation. Polly, such forgivingness is a mere dry word, a virtuous excuse for hating. I forgive you if

you're unjust; you forgive me if I'm in fault;
and so—farewell all, and never speak again;
but so pass each other by in the narrow
streets that one would swear, had we not
said friends, that we were sworn enemies. Is
it to be so?"

Age had not yet proofed Polly against so
much earnestness, and she could hardly falter,

"I do not know, and it doesn't lie with
me to decide."

"Nay, Polly," he entreated, offering to
stay her.

"I cannot stop, sir," she replied. "Besides, yonder are some of our village girls
coming from the ferry, and it's not well
spoken of, if girls like me are seen talking to
gentlemen."

In fact forms could be dimly perceived by
Humphrey to advance from that direction,
laughing and singing some catch as they
went.

"*Honi soit qui mal y pense*," he answered
warmly. "There are gentlemen yet in England who are honourable, and village girls
who are born gentle."

Polly turned to go, but not soon enough,

for she had been descried, and was now hailed by a chorus of girlish voices. Too late to avoid them she stayed her steps, saying to Humphrey—

" You had better leave me, sir."

Somewhat grudging he made as if to go, but only stepped into the deep gloom of the two great elms that fronted the inn, and there stopped to watch the issue.

CHAPTER VII.

ON came the girls trooping, some dozen of
them, laughing, shouting, and singing—

> Where, O where's the kiss I gen ye
>   Yisterday, Jack?
> Fower thief, I did't but len ye;
>   Gie't me back.
> Come here or anywhere,
> Come now or anyhow,
>   And gie't me back.

A parcel of rough, healthy, country lasses
they were, with not an ounce of hypochondriac
diffidence among them, having little intuition
of good, and perhaps no great commission of
evil. So they clustered round Polly noisily
greeting her.

"What, Polly," cried one of them breathless, "won't you speak to us?"

"You're proud now, are you?" said
another.

"And why should I be proud, Sally?"
said Polly.

At this all the girls looked as knowing as
they could in the dark, and burst into laughter.

WISE OR OTHERWISE. 95

"Because," answered Sally, "you've got a young man at last. We saw him."

"O, yes, we saw him!" shouted the rest.

"Why," said Polly, "you are not proud, Sally, with half a dozen of them."

"O, but I'm used to it, you see," answered Sally loftily.

"I believe you'd get used to cholera," said Polly, laughing in spite of anxiety.

"Oh, Polly," cried one and another of the girls, "you're sly, too, are you? Where is he? I saw him! Tell us who he is. What's his name?"

But Polly refusing to satisfy them—

"Let's find him!" they begin to cry. "He can't be far away! Hunt him out, hunt him out."

So off they fly, scampering about like a herd of unbroken fillies, until a pair of sharp eyes discovers Humphrey quaking in the deepest of the gloom, trapped in a corner, with no way of escape.

"I spy, I spy!" she hallos.

"Found, found!" they shout, flocking up.

What could Humphrey do but stand where he was, put up his coat-collar and pull down his hat, devoutly hoping he might not be recognised? Mad with excitement, the girls danced round him with joined hands, singing their catch. It would have been useless to fume, and so he waits patiently, putting as good a face as he can on a foolish body, until the maidens are tired of their gambols. Then he politely bows with as bold an air as the oldest robber of the band, saying—

"Delighted to meet you here so merry, ladies."

At which they have no better grace than to laugh loud and long.

"Many thanks for the charming concert with *ballet divertissement* that you have favoured me with."

Alas, far from courteously accepting his compliments, they only laughed the more.

"Ha-ha-ha," he continues with a very fair imitation of a laugh, "we can't do better than laugh while our teeth are good."

They all laughed again, oh, so heartily, as if they had never laughed before. The rugged elms were cheered to hear them, and the old Trent chuckled aloud.

"All your teeth are good, I see," said the young gentleman.

"O yes," answered the most forward of the girls, "we can all bite."

"Like dogs," said another. "Bow-wow."

The whole troop repeated to the echo —

"Bow-wow! bow-wow!"

"Bravo!" said Humphrey, clapping his hands. "As well done as if you were all pugs."

"And we can scratch, too, like cats," cried a third. "Mew!"

"Mew-mew!" responded the others, clawing with their hands.

"Well said," applauded Humphrey, "very well said, indeed."

O, how they laughed! They laughed as it would do you good to hear them; they laughed as if laughing were their trade.

"Now let's take him up to Polly," cried one malicious tongue; and the proposal was hailed with acclamation.

When Polly saw Humphrey taken, being free for a while, she had taken the opportunity to escape, but soon returned as though she had voted it base to forsake her fellow-sufferer in the hour of trial.

H

"Go, sir, go," she whispered aside to him, as he was led up to her; "I am used to their rough ways."

Taking her trembling hand, and putting his head close to her downcast face, as the lasses skipt wildly about them, he replied—

"Dearest, this can neither hurt nor shame us, if we're resolved that it shall not."

"I cannot bear," she faltered, "to see you so mocked."

"Dearest," he answered again, "I am brazen-proof; and have no fear that any disgrace shall arrive on you through me."

> Where, O where's the kiss I gen ye
>   Yisterday, Jack?
> Fower thief I did 't but len ye;
>   Gie't me back.
> Come here or anywhere,
> Come now or anyhow,
>   An' gie't me back.

So sang the maidens again and again, until Humphrey was fain to cry—

"Well, if you challenge me so boldly and so often, kiss you I must although to another name."

So saying, he caught one or two of the nearest damsels and heartily bussed them;

whereupon the whole troop fled, vanquished, shrieking and laughing and clinging to one another.

Quit of those gnats, Humphrey had leisure to return to his companion, to whom he drew so near that he could see how moved she was.

" Are you angry Polly ? " he asked.

" Only," she answered, " because I seem to have disgraced you."

" I am disgraced," quoth he, " only if you are, which cannot be. But I shall be miserable, if you make me a part of your displeasure."

" Are you not vexed ? "

" How can I be, Polly, at what brought me nearer to you than I have ever been before ? "

He was hesitating, on the brink of saying more, when Polly took up the word, saying—

"I had better follow the girls. Unless I overtake them, I shall never overtake their tongues."

She started to go, but found the young man still by her side.

"No," she said firmly; "I must go alone."

" Do you command that ?" asked Hum-phrey.

" I have no right to command, sir; I can only venture to wish."

" Your wish is my command," replied he, " more than the statute-book. I wish you would always command me."

" You would soon tire," quoth she, " of such an entertainment; the novelty would scarcely survive three askings."

" Do you think so, Polly ? Make the ex-periment now on this vile body."

Still walking on, she replied more lightly—

" I have heard of persons with a passion for command; you may be one. Good-bye, sir."

" Good-night, not good-bye," he pleaded. " Give me but one more opportunity. I have been either very wicked or very unfortunate, and don't know as yet whether to repent of my sins or tax my fortune. Will you meet me to-morrow morning at the first stile in the grove ?"

" I think I should not," murmured Polly, unable, in the tumult of her thoughts, to balance considerations.

" Only for once, I promise you. You will? At nine o'clock ? "

Eager to be gone, feverishly endeavouring to consider calmly, what could she say ?

" I will come if—"

" You will? Thank you, Polly," cried the young man, ignoring the if; and Polly was constrained or content to leave it so.

" Good-night, Polly," was Humphrey's farewell, as she sped away. " Think of me to-night, and remember me to-morrow."

Polly sped away, and her lover remained behind, sitting on one of the many stiles that guard the river footpath. And as he sat he was thinking as follows, but with more diffusiveness than dare be shown in print. For is it not true, my readers, that our self-communings are apt to be very weak, very selfish, very maudlin; full of regret, empty of foresight; grabbing pleasure, spewing at the noblest pain; pitiful as a drunkard's hiccup? No; we should wrong our friend in exposing him at his weakest, if we published all that was passing through his mind; like Noah's dove, let us hope, to find no resting-place there. This, then, is the better substance of his thoughts—

"So she goes off with a smile, or almost; with the May promise of a smile between her lips, like a scented bud with the dew on it in the morning; an angel smile not yet made flesh, but wooing so sweet a delivery." With much more anent her smiles and eyes and voice, and every perfection. "I could hardly withhold my most ardent words, as she stood so beautiful before me; but I have a prior duty. My mother shall have my humblest words to-night. I see that I have been wrong, grievously wrong. And see how so late? By the light of Polly's eyes, I am like a child coaxed with sweetmeats and caresses to do my best and freest pleasure. But my eyes were shut and I did not see."

Just so, my friend, our white-robed duties become more visible when they are coloured with pleasure or advantage.

Later in the night, Humphrey found himself strolling in the neighbourhood of the Berridges' cottage; and, naturally enough, for the evening was pleasant, the air good, and the scenery beautiful under the rising moon. Beside which he had nothing else to do, bating an engagement which he had forgotten. He had been there some time enjoying the air and so forth, when he was hailed by the sturdy voice of Mike, coming home from work.

After the usual greetings, the lad, dropping his voice, and taking off his hat, so as to scratch his head more easily in his difficulties, began to say—

"Do you know, Mr. Humphrey, I don't think things are quite square at home. I dunno how 'tis, but something's out o' gear. Trade's good, you know; and if 'twere bad, why it's like the rain, we're used to it. I wish you'd come down sometime and see father, and—make him out."

"Are you quite sure," said Mr. Humphrey, fishing with ground bait, "that he would be glad to see me in his trouble?"

"If he ain't, I tell you what, sir, he's awfully bad. And mother'd be happy to see you. And me too, as far as that goes, if I'm any account."

"And Polly too, eh?" said Humphrey, jocularly. "Why don't you finish the list?"

But Mike was unaccountably silent, and Humphrey began to doubt.

" Come, what about Polly ? Is it a secret ?"

No question that the boy was at a loss, and Humphrey became still more alarmed.

" She wouldn't be beyond measure delighted ? " said Humphrey again more bitterly, as mocking himself while he accused others. " Speak the truth, Mike ! "

And speak he did at last, reluctantly but honestly, and showing embarrassment in his bristly hair, his downcast face, his twisted arms, and in his feet shuffling uneasily and spurning every pebble within reach.

" Why you know, sir, gells are gells."

" Well ?"

" And queer uns too enough."

" Well ? "

" And Polly's a gell, though she's an uncommon 'un."

" Well ? " again said Humphrey sharply, still refusing to help him out.

" Well—I dunno," answered Mike from the slough of despond, unable to set foot backwards or forwards.

" You only mean that Polly isn't quite out of mind with joy at seeing me ?"

" Why—well—you see—"

" Just so."

" Gells will be gells, sir; they can't help themselves. Bless you, I know a lot of 'em; not that they're to be compared with Polly, either, though she is a gell, and that can't be denied. Oh, their heads are full o' whims. Why there's our Polly, she'll talk nonsense by the yard as beautiful as print, like the Arabian Nights. Oh, she'll come round, sir, she'll come round."

So spoke Mike, warming as he proceeded, and comforting himself in trying to comfort Humphrey.

" Won't you come in with me?"

" I think not to-night."

The boy was going, but the backwash of his uneasiness returning on him, he stopped to say—

" You don't mind, sir, that about Polly?"

" Oh, not at all, not at all," answered Humphrey, wincing, but grimly careless.

" That's right," said Mike, now quite recovered. " Good-night, sir. I daresay she didn't mean it. Good-night."

" Stay, Mike, don't think I'm offended, but I have a little curiosity; simply that.

Tell me honestly whether this feeling of hers has come up lately or no."

" Well, no, sir," answered Mike, suffering a slight relapse of doubt, " I can't say it has. Oh, it's only a whim that's grown up with her, and she'll put it by some day like her doll."

" That is all.   Don't think that I am at all displeased.   Good-night."

So Mike turned happily in, leaving Humphrey to amuse himself as he could with his thoughts.

" So I was after all a poor deluded fool? Nay, rather am I not now a poor undeluded fool, formerly rich in a million of delusions, now beggared of all?"

Yes, the aspects of the game had changed. He feared to lose by an odd point, and now finds himself nowhere; he has not scored one.

" Might he be mistaken? No, he is too happy to see what does not exist, and too honest to say what he does not believe. Besides, this explains all; it fits too easily into the puzzle to be anything but the missing piece.   He shut his eyes and thought himself invisible. Yes, they have looked me through like a transparency, and would tend my interests in spite of myself. But she hinted at some grave fault. There is something still behind this revelation. But what matter, what matter? Another truth will not eat this up."

Quite right, my friend Humphrey; when all the treasure is stolen, what care for sundries? Since all your fortunes are shipwrecked, why waste tears over particular losses?

"The main fact remains that she does not love me; and I had better go and think of some other lady."

*　　*　　*　　*　　*　　*

Polly found an opportunity to speak alone with her father, as she was bidding him good-night. With much hesitation she began—

"Father, I saw Mr. Humphrey to-night in the road."

"Eh?" said the old man, showing little gratification.

"I couldn't help it, you know."

Polly was disheartened from saying more; but after a pause, Amos asked her—

" Did he speak to thee ? "

" Ye—es," answered Polly ; who would certainly have been rebuked by her mother, had she been present, for round shoulders. "I couldn't help that, you know."

" Ah," said her father, thoughtfully rubbing his chin, and said no more.

It was sometime before Polly plucked up courage to continue timidly—

" He spoke very kindly, father."

" No doubt. You must be careful, my lass."

" I will, father. He seemed very innocent, and spoke most kindly."

" Be very careful, my lass."

" I will, father. I spoke coldly to him, but he was very gentle in his reply."

Polly waited, but Amos seemed to find much matter for thought, none for talk.

" He asked me to meet him again ; only for once, he promised."

" And did you consent ? " the father asked, with something of fear in his tones.

" I was hurried—I had no time to refuse. I said I would if—"

" If what, my child ? "

"I only said if—" Polly replied, trying to smile and not weep; "he stopped me there. I meant if you thought well of it, father; I couldn't have any condition but that. To-morrow morning, he asked me, at nine o'clock."

"You'd better not go, Polly, my lass. No good 'll come that way that can't come other ways."

Polly swallowed down whatever ought not to appear, with no sighs or tears or chokings at the throat, but looking bravely and speaking boldly.

"Very well, father, I won't see him. Good-night."

So saying, she kissed him, and took up her candle to go.

"Stay, my lass," cried Amos, rising to stop her; "thou'rt a honour to me and to this house. Go if thee will; I can trust thee."

"Nay, father, not against your pleasure."

"Yes, go, lass, go. Thee 'll take a good heart there, and can't bring a bad 'un back."

* * * * * *

The same evening Humphrey also had a

communication with his mother ; letting her know after a heavy attempt at lightness, a sort of patriarchal levity, that he wished to travel. With a yearning at heart she enquired, How was that ? O, the whim had taken him. Had she any objection ? Not if he had any desire. Ah, yes, self-abnegation is the mother's part ; while her children feed in infancy on her breast, in age on her every comfort. Where did he wish to go ? To which he was understood to answer, anywhere ; all places were much alike. In spite of a growing tenderness that inclined her to burst into tears and throw herself on her son's neck, she merely said—

"Very well. When do you wish to start ?"

"To-morrow, if I can ; if not the next day, or the next."

Manifestly he was very unhappy. What had happened ? Things that Paul had mentioned darted across her mind, but were instantly beaten back by her proud integrity, that stood like a bulwark against things ignoble. Should she make one more attempt on his heart ? Ay, and say with fond solicitude—

" Nothing more, Humphrey ? "

But certain resolutions of his made in another climate were forgotten amid that weather tempestuous ; he was at war, when peace treaties are null. Without reply he rose to go ; but as soon as he touched the door-handle, he made haste to return. Had he resolved in the nick of time to tell her all ? Yes. No, he only kissed her forehead ; he would speak to-morrow—perhaps.

CHAPTER VIII.

THE next morning by eight o'clock Polly was sitting in the garden, cheerfully engaged at her lace-mending, and even at times singing merry snatches, a habit that she had dropped of late.

> Merrily the ship goes,
> While the wind blows ;
> When it is still,
> The more repose.

Mike, as he passes out, stops to listen to the music that he loves. When she has finished the stanza, he goes up to her and puts his big rough hands on her shoulder, and meeting the face that turned up to his with a look of proud love, asks somewhat anxiously—

" Are you all right, Polly ? eh, faithfully ? "

" Yes," she replies laughing, " I'm as well as can be expected."

Even his keen espial can descry nothing but content on her face, so he kisses and leaves her ; but turning back with a sudden remembrance asks—

"Now why, Polly, don't you like Mr. Humphrey?"

Polly, with a pretty blush that will not look up and show itself, replies—

"I don't know, I'm sure, why I shouldn't like him. But shan't you be late for work?"

"I s'pose I'd better be off," says he, "but it's queer enough, too."

So off he goes, dubiously pondering the riddle, while his sister takes up her song again.

> Merrily the mill goes,
> While the brook flows;
> When it is still,
> The more repose.

Old Berridge, too, hears and is glad; for he puts his head out of the window to hearken.

"What, singing, lass? singing again?"

"Yes, father."

"That's well, that's well."

So saying, he withdrew his head to attend to business, while his daughter continued her song.

> Merrily the world goes,
> While dear love glows;
> When it is still,
> The more repose.

The saucy words were barely uttered, when

I

she took up a tenderer strain in a favourite ballad that she had discovered somewhere, and sang to any tune that ran in her head.

> Tell me, where is the hoarded wealth,
>   And mighty health,
>   And happiness?
> In dear love's poverty,
>   In dear love's deep distress,
> In dear love's malady.

Here old Berridge looked out of the window again, saying—

"The heart's in no bad plight, when there's singing in 't, eh, lass?"

"No, father," she responded cheerily.

"That's well."

> Tell me where is constancy,
>   Prosperity,
>   And steady faith?
> In dear love's turnabouts,
>   In dear love's bitter scaith,
> In dear love's changing doubts.

Mrs. Berridge, too, clattering in and out and to and fro on household matters, is pleased with the sound but finds nothing to say. Indeed does not know that it is necessary to say anything; being one of those rough-finished persons that are dumb to their tenderest emotions, however voluble their tongues to scold and gossip; esteemed, therefore, a shallow sort by those who have much to say on everything. Mrs. Berridge takes the music like the sunshine without a word. Pleased she is, but whether she knows how, whether she even thinks about it, I cannot undertake to say.

> Tell me, where is upright truth,
> And melting ruth,
>   And liberty?
> In dear love's knavery,
>   In dear love's cruelty,
> In dear love's slavery.

Hallo, now comes Mike back in hot haste. He lays a letter on Polly's lap, saying breathlessly that Mr. Humphrey had just met him and given it him for her.

"Shan't you open it?" he cried, astonished to see it lie. "I will, then!"

"No thank you, Mike," said Polly, quietly retaining it. "I must finish this hole first."

"There you go, Polly!" he rejoined, much grieved. "It's the queerest thing!"

He cannot find heart to blame her, but Fate.

Alas! poor Fate, you bear the ass's pack.

"I'll back if 't had been from old Aunt Mary and her cat, you'd ha' torn it open and read it six times by this; and from Mr.

Humphrey! There it goes into your pocket, and like as not you 'll forget all about it, and p'raps an answer wanted. Bless my life if I ain't lecturing you! But why can't you bear him, Polly? I believe he likes you uncommon. I came across him only last night, and—whew—"

He had nearly put his foot in it, but stopped in time with a whistle—that expression of a boy's inexpressible.

"And what, Mike?"

"Why," answered Mike, as if a tooth were being drawn with each word, "he said—I mean—I said—but," with a sudden brilliant thought, "it's time I was back at work. Good-bye."

He being gone, Polly has leisure, though the hole is yet unfinished, to open the note and read :—

"My dear Polly, I am very sorry that it is impossible for me to meet you this morning. Please to excuse me; and when I ask you for another appointment, I will permit nothing to break it.

"HUMPHREY DENTON."

Polly, being little experienced in epistolary style, dwelt much upon that impossible, and found relief therein.

" He would have come, if it had been possible ; and in that assurance lies the comfort and substance of a meeting. And if it had been possible ? He pleaded with such a begging eye, that he must have something of moment to communicate. ' I am very sorry.' If he is very sorry, then I am little sorry ; though that sounds unkind."

Ah, inexperienced Polly ! So little does her heart forbode, that she is even ready to finish her song.

Tell me, where is tied affection,
Free election,
   Pure content ?
In dear love's angry mood,
   And self abandonment,
And fond solicitude.

Tell me, where simplicity,
Humility,
   And cleanness bide ?
In dear love's wily art,
   In dear love's loving pride,
In dear love's every part."

" Encore, encore," cried a voice over the hedge ; and an unwelcome one too, for it was Mr. Chatterly's. " Bravo, Polly ! "

Polly made no response, but hastily turned her chair round.

Chatterly was now lolling over the gate, and cried, " Why do you give me your back, Polly ? "

She was tempted to answer, "Because you have face enough of your own," but refrained.

In quick time Mrs. Berridge strides out, calling shrilly, "Put on that hat, you wicked girl, unless you want to catch your death of cold! I'm to be always at you, am I ?"

Polly donned her hat, and Chatterly slunk away, inwardly saying, " Humph, the *mater*. I don't like her style! She looks equal to pulling all my hair out to make a front for herself."

There was nothing for him but to pass down the village, and amuse himself with whistling and flicking pebbles with his stick, occasionally turning round on his heels to— to warm them for aught I know.

But what is it that comes fluttering through Berridge's gate ? Polly's shawl and Polly under it ; and both together glide up Clifton road. Here is a chance for Mr. Chatterly, and he turns back at once to take advantage of it. Following her at a discreet distance as she walks quietly along, he manages to keep her in sight. She calls at no house, but passes through the village, and then, leaving the road, enters Clifton Grove.

"Ah, that's your game, is it?" thought Chatterly. "I can beat you at that."

He waited until she was fairly among the trees, and then running some distance down the road, struck quickly through the fields, so as to gain a march on the girl, who was sauntering leisurely along.

But what was she doing out in work-hours, since that engagement was broken? A foolish little whim, I suppose, to keep her part, though the best of it was impossible. She would walk down to the stile, and there having rested awhile, return the more content.

CHAPTER IX.

How it was that, shortly before the appointed time, Humphrey showed himself in the appointed place he could not himself have said. It was scarcely by intention, not altogether in unconsciousness. And if he wished to avoid Polly, what better place than that, where she had no business even of fancy? Anyhow a pleasanter spot to be miserable in could hardly be chosen. The disconsolate lover, perched on the stile, might look down the irregular line of elms that border the river as far as Wilford; or if he turned, he could not but gaze long upon the thick grove that nobly adorns the steep ascent to Clifton.

How the place tempts both the unhappy and the comfortable, as it did Humphrey, to lie down here by the river's brink under the light shadow of a clump of hawthorns. To lie on one's back thoughtlessly, and watch the high-floating clouds, the busy fluttering insects, and the rustling leaves; dreamily remembering, dreamily forgetting, until even sorrow is unsubstantial, and nothing but ease and peace and sleep lives. To lie on our mother's lap, looking into our father's face, while we are lulled to forget the bauble that we cried for, and at last sink back on those strong arms, that gentle bosom, and rest.

But no rest will last but the last; and Humphrey's is broken by Chatterly, carolling as he takes the stile—

> Do you want to know the smartest lass,
> As lives in this here port?
> Why that's my Polly, the lively Polly,
> And she's a rare good sort.

Humphrey hears, but will not trouble himself to look; in fact hopes to escape unseen, his present mood not being for such a companion. The gay intruder, however, catches sight of a stray boot, and being of an inquisitive turn, passes softly round the bushes, and, unnoticed, takes full account of its wearer.

"You, is it?" thinks he to himself. "I'll soon smoke you out."

Whereupon with sly designs he returns to the stile, and seats himself on it, humming—

> For Polly, she's so jolly!

"Ah, yes," says he, somewhat louder than a stage whisper, more like a deaf man talking to himself; "this is the spot. Dear Polly!"

At this Humphrey pricks up his ears.

"This, the very stile that she perched her lovely self on. I kiss it, hoping it didn't cut her."

Humphrey raises himself on his elbows, and throws his head forward to listen the better.

"This is the very rail that she scraped her pretty thick boots on:

For Polly, she's so jolly!"

This was all very absurd, but still maddening to one who was mad before.

"Ay, that's the very post that she dangled her hat on. I throw it a blessing to catch if it can; I never could."

Humphrey was now on his feet.

"This is the very arm that entwined her little waist. Sweet Polly!"

This was really too much to bear, even though the false secrets were only uttered to the old trees, that were shaking and muttering underbreath, like teethless cronies, delivering who knows what. This allusion to the waist was really too much to bear, false as it was.

"And these the very lips that—"

"You lie!" cried Humphrey, boldly confronting the traducer.

Chatterly laughed loud.

"Hahaha! Polly she's so jolly! Hahaha! Only a hint at lips, and you rush round like Don Domino charging Sir Hippodrome with a clothes' prop. Hahaha! For Polly she's so jolly! Isn't she?"

"Every Polly rhymes to jolly," answered Humphrey, in no good humour.

"I deny it. Our Polly's jolly, and there's never another Polly that rhymes to her. Shall we go halves, or toss? Now then, heads or tails for Polly that's so jolly; the only Polly that never rhymes to melancholy or any folly but what's jolly. Sharp, before she's here."

"Before she's here?" said Humphrey. "What do you mean?"

"Don't be so sly," answered the other, missing the mark at his wisest like most of us; "it's impudent to call me a fool, and you can't be so knowing without engrossing all the wisdom present."

Humphrey looked round, and there sure enough was Polly coming quietly along; but her hands were busy knitting, and her thoughts far away, trespassing on who knows what forbidden grounds, so that she did not perceive the young men. The surprise overthrew the balance of Humphrey's common sense, and he said hastily—

"You're mistaken if you think I expected to see her. In fact I must be gone; I have an engagement," taking out his watch, "and by Jove! it's nine o'clock, time that I was there."

According to his genius, believing nothing of this, Chatterly laughingly seized him by the coat, saying—

"Nay, nay, come; stay, if only to keep me in countenance. Hi, Polly, here's one of your admirers playing false."

However, he managed to break away from his tormentor, clear the stile, and gain the cover of the trees before the girl's attention was aroused; while Chatterly laughed until he was fain to hang upon the fence.

" Up to the neck in fun ! I shall drown ! I shall drown ! "

Meanwhile the knitter had approached, and then only looked up and saw with disgust with whom she had to deal.

Up strode he, manifesting a swaggering admiration, wherein he admired himself much more.

" You're too late for Denton, Polly, so you may as well stay with me. He has gone; rushed off at sight of your pretty face, like a bull at a bit of red."

" You would be quite as funny, sir, if you were more truthful. I know that Mr. Denton is not here," quoth Polly, and showed her back to his undesirable company.

" Quite so," answered he, following step by step; " he has just run away on a par ticular engagement at nine o'clock, by Jove ! With Miss Manlove, I believe."

Polly turned full upon him, saying—

" Sir, that is not true," taking her stand there just as Humphrey, repenting of his cowardice, and fearing that his absence would be an unscrupulous rival's too great advan tage, began to return.

" Well," continued Chatterly, " I'll bet two kisses to one on it, Polly."

" I know that it is impossible," she replied.

" Will you take the odds, then ? You daren't ? "

" I dare," she answered boldly, " if it were necessary."

" Done ! I found him sneaking behind those trees. You'll see his footmarks there if you go."

Polly only shook her head and again offered to depart; she would not even pretend to doubt. Neither of them saw Humphrey, who was walking quietly upon the grass under the big elms.

Meanwhile Chatterly was trying to persuade Polly with all those paltry arts that men of his stamp never believe ineffectual, even when they find them so. He leered, he postured, he took her arm, which was indignantly withdrawn; he offered her words barely heard, no whit heeded.

How far he was from her heart, Mr. Chatterly, that lady-popular man, little dreamt. How far? The twain could not live in the same climate—same hemisphere—could not breathe the same atmosphere. Their very organs of life differed; hers fashioned for the celestial ether, clear and serene; his for the grovelling fog, dull, fat and earthy.

Now Humphrey had climbed the stile, not desiring, hardly shunning observation; and, unseen, was coming round the clump towards them, when Chatterly, unable to persuade the girl to go with him, strode by himself to the place, hoping that she would follow. To his astonishment, he again confronted his rival.

" Why, here he is again, like a Jack-in-the box."

Polly was hurrying away, but at that call looked round, and for a moment stood before her speechless lover, then hastened from the place where she had been so much unde-ceived. Chatterly hied after her, laughing at the mischief.

" Pay the stakes, Polly. Nothing like ready money. Now that isn't honest, Polly. I won't be done, you little welsher."

This was more than Humphrey could bear. He rushed forward and thrust himself be-tween the maid and her persecutor, crying—

" Let her be. Keep off, you scoundrel ! "

" Not for you," fiercely retorted Chatterly, clenching his fist into a natural argument ; " not for you, you confounded sneak. Get up your tree."

He throws himself past the self-enlisted guard, but is pushed violently back, near measuring his length. With an effort he keeps his feet ; and now had war raged between the champions had not Polly, at first affrighted, now interposed with indignant mien and resolute, uplifted hand.

" What are you doing, men ? " she cried. " Do you call this your courage, or your evil passions ? If you would be law-breakers, cannot you choose a better time and easier way than to quarrel about me, who have no interest in either of you ? Have you no strength, no wisdom, but in your fingers ? "

The two strong men stood to be chidden like naughty children, and had not a word to answer.

" Mr. Chatterly, if you think yourself anything better than the common people to whom I belong, you will go at once the way that I point."

" That isn't fair, Polly," said Chatterly, trying to ogle her and glare at Humphrey at the same time. " You ought to order him off, too."

" I shall ask him to go the other way."

" And go with him yourself. Of course he won't refuse."

" I shall not do that."

" Then you must follow me ; there's no other way. Well, Polly, I don't want to annoy you, though I should like to finish off that eaves-dropping scamp. You shall keep the kiss at interest, and give me a private settling day."

So he retreated, whistling a careless defiance of his foe, to whom Polly turned resolutely.

" Now, sir, the other way, if you will please to pardon a command."

With difficulty he said—

" First hear me, Polly."

" No, sir," she answered ; " I have heard you speak too much, whether for my ears or your honesty."

" No, Polly ; I may have troubled you with wearisome, never dishonest talk. But

K

you are in haste to be after yon fellow, and settle kisses with him."

"I shall not care to answer your jibe, if you will only leave me."

"I go, I go," he said moodily. And he did go as far as the stile, laid a hesitating hand on it, stopped, suddenly returned.

"And did you," he asked, "receive my note?"

"I did," she replied.

The next words were harder still to speak.

"And were you so kind, nevertheless, as to come and meet me?"

"No, sir, indeed," she answered indignantly, many things fighting in her mind, "and did not hope to see you."

"There lies the cause," he retorted, glad to be bitter; "you can't brook to see me unexpected; that's a sight that needs preparation."

"The happening of an impossibility," she replied, "might well fall on me strangely and suddenly."

"Come, you took the word in too large a meaning."

"I was largely mistaken; it means little.

You do not go, sir. Mr. Chatterly, whom
you despise, esteemed my desire more
courteously."

"It is not in him," cried Humphrey
warmly; "his courtesies are bribes, and not
loyal tribute. But if I intrude, Polly, if you
have made another appointment and a better
this way—"

" By what right," she exclaimed, "do you
ask? Am I not free? I don't pry into
your reasons for coming here. Had I the
wish, I have not the license to be so curious.
But if it were so, I should at least have
expected to find the ground empty of
espiage."

His bitterness stunned, knocked on the
head by amazement—

"Am I spy?" he said. "Well, I lack
self-assertion to refuse the basest name
offered; though that is unkinder than I
thought you had any knowledge of; cata-
logued amongst the things for which you had
no word, only a silence."

Polly again answered, her wrath rising as
she uttered it, while all the evil that she had
heard of the young man before her, all the

wickednesses she had knowledge or concep-
tion of, rushed to her mind and printed there
each a copy of its horrors.

"No, sir," she said, "and there are other
things that we could pronounce at will,
though never so ill-instructed. Ignorance is
learned enough to spell what it sees; it can
read baseness's name in its own slime."

But Humphrey was astounded beyond
anger, little suspecting the source whence
those fierce words flowed.

"I am base? Everything vile must be
written on my name? My character a common blank wall for every boy's, every passer's
abuse?"

"That," she replied, already beginning to
relent from the havoc she had made, "could
not be, if you were innocent."

"O, there you err!" beset with ignorant,
unknown accusations, so he replied. "What
is of least avail in the world's assaults is innocence. Nothing is so easily taken unawares,
nothing so tamely ensnared, nothing plucked
so close. Its weapons and defence are a
fable; damage and distress touch it all
over."

"Ah," she replied, "if you had known innocence you'd have known it not so feeble; but to those who are not friends, she comes in the night only. Or if it be true, why, what a caution is here to beware of—others, and make as cunning of my safety as a partridge. Your warning was given earnestly, I hope meant truly, and I will accept it frankly."

So saying she turns away from him and all his excuses, and makes for Wilford; but Humphrey called after her, " Do not depart, Polly, if you desire to stay. My presence shall distress you neither now nor hereafter."

With this he sprung the stile, and hastened Cliftonwards, never looking back, and was soon lost among the trees. Polly had stopped at his words, and stood watching his retreat, maybe regretting her sharp and angry speeches, or hoping for his return ; still in these debates the tongue will be speaking crueller words than the heart warrants. We flourish edged tools though we would not kill. For even amid the bitterest thoughts who knows what tenderness lies, and how much love intermixed with hate? But there was no hatred in Polly's heart nor much anger, when she had lost sight of the form that she expected never to see again so happily. Recording many vows and forgetting much unkindness, she went heavily homewards.

CHAPTER X.

Sometimes, even in the company of the live-
liest talkers, a dead pause will fall, and grow
from unnoticed nothing, like a giant's brat,
stronger by moments, until the most wanton
wit is abashed, the most voluble tongue over-
crowed; and all sit under the mystery like a
group overtaken in Pompeii. At length
some desperate wretch startles them with a
whisper of nothing, whereupon they draw
breath, look round, take their ease, and begin
to talk again quietly. But what, you ask, is
that here? Why, a pretty simile.

*   *   *   *   *

It happened in the afternoon following the
events recorded in the last chapter, that Mr.
Gray presented himself at Mrs. Denton's.
He was dressed with even more care than
ordinary; his hat without a hair turned, linen
stiff in pride of conscious purity, gloves un-
dimmed, boots very blackamoor suns, his
coat and trousers a marvel of old-fashioned

art; in short, most like a superannuated beau, whose years have glided by too fast for his leisurely pace, and left him too old or careless to overtake them. We have memorials in stone that some call pathetic, and even weep over, but there are sadder relics in flesh and blood, standing solitary in days to which they were not born.

Mrs. Denton was at home, and after a while appeared, and welcomed her visitor heartily.

"I fear," said he, "that my call is inopportune."

"No," she answered, "I can rarely be so circumstanced that a visit of yours is unseasonable."

They sat down, and Mr. Gray continued—"Yes, we have known each other long."

"All our lives," answered the lady. "I learnt to recognise you before I had any acquaintance with myself, and each experience of my life has only been another passage in our friendship. We played together in childhood, laughed and frolicked in youth, and now talk together sedately, like good elderly folk."

"Have you indeed grown old," said the

gentleman, "and lost the spirit of youth? To my eyes you seem as young, or at least as fully blest with all wherein youth is good and beautiful, as on May the twelfth in twenty-eight."

"My wedding-day," she cried. "You remember that? and yet complain of a memory constantly insolvent, saying that it borrows right and left, and on the day makes a composition of twopence in the pound. No, I am no longer young, even in appearance. My fortieth year is behind me; and what is that but youth past; impatience, peevish babe, rocked asleep with the cradling swell of the years; my friends and relations dead, lost, aged; my husband taken from me; crosses borne, mercies endured; and I am not touched? Yes, but fatherly."

"You have no age for me," he said; "you were venerable in youth, and are and will be fresh and youthful in middle life and old age."

Mr. Gray drew his chair a little closer, and as Mrs. Denton, occupied with her thoughts, did not look up, ventured for a moment to touch with his own the hand that rested on her knee.

"Let me confide to you a story of my past life, that is its history, and all my present and future too. I once loved a lady."

Mrs. Denton now turned her eyes upon him, and did not withdraw them.

"I had known her long; but whether my love was too deep to be eager, too devout to be importunate, or whether I lacked the eloquent ability to make expression significant, or whether it was fear or merely procrastination, I made it secret, until a better man came with a better tongue, and, having dared to woo, won her. But after twenty long, happy years, during which I, who was always Gray, grew grayer, the husband departed, vacating the kingship, curtailing the happiness of a wide circle, and then I, the earlier lover came—Do not let me grieve you."

For she had hidden her face away.

"But I am grieved," she replied.

"No more then," said he, striving to be cheerful against a quavering voice, "no more. A more urgent matter, a younger trouble claims my mention."

"Dear friend," answered the lady, resting her hand on his arm, and regarding him with

a sisterly face, " dear friend, let a dear friendship suffice. I have had a husband worthy of
a widowhood. If there can be any other
compensation for being so long a sorrow to
you, I should be happier."

" No need, dear lady," he answered, man-
fully cheerful at last. " My recollections—
or what would to others be recollections—I
have never forgotten—that past-in-present is
my old, crabbed, well-accustomed crony. We
live together, sit, eat, and drink together at
the same board, sleep in the same bed, and
wake together with the same mind to breakfast. I did not hope for any return but the
return of some friendliness ; but to have a
long silent love of such a quality as this
never hear itself but die in silence, so great
a self-renunciation was beyond me. Or if
another reason is needed for a story so out of
date, let it serve to demonstrate with how
active a stamp in our waxen age love im-
presses us."

" I knew it before," said Mrs. Denton,
sorrowfully, " and now see it too well."

Mr. Gray persisted.

" Imperiously it manages, aye, the starkest

and proudest of us, either for our damage or our advancement."

"Dear friend," again said Mrs. Denton, "I know it, and I grieve for you."

"I do not speak of myself," he replied; "as I have said, there is now no more sorrow for me but your sorrows. Tell me, what is a wife's best quality?"

"How can you ask me, who have been an imperfect wife, to bring out the standard of perfection that I stand short of?"

"Tell me, and do not fear the comparison."

"Doubtless the fear and love of God, and all which that brings."

"Such as uprightness, purity, trust, candour, charity, mercy, unselfishness, gentleness, virtue?"

"Those are the names, but where, alas! are the forms?"

"I might reply, but it matters not. These conjoined to beautiful personal endowments and a fineness of spirit that no want of instruction could dull—"

"No want of instruction?" said the lady surprised, as she well might be. "What is this?"

"I do not say I perceived any poverty of knowledge; unless a certain decorous simplicity be accounted ignorance."

Mr. Gray stopped, and seemed to look for a word from his listener; so perforce she said almost coldly, "I shall not recognise the lady unless you name her."

Ah, by how little a hole suspicion will enter the serenest natures!

"Do not misjudge me," he answered, with a touching emphasis that ashamed the lady; "there is no pattern of excellence for me but one. A young friend whose father I could wish to be, to whom indeed I am a kind of father, a father and friend too—not as some parents at once feared and disobeyed—he has admitted me into council even with his love, and I have taken pains to be able to give him direct and fatherly advice. If the truth be told, I shall deem him happy in his love when he is successful, and not unhappy now, though he is perplexed and anxious. Dearest lady, if you had a son, and if he were bound to an affection of such a colour and proportion as that, would you not rather strengthen the union than cut him loose from so much goodness?"

"You speak in riddles," was the unresponsive answer.

"Easily guessed. Dearest lady, do not entertain a proud nice adherence to formalities, refusing to perceive what you see, refusing to understand what you know. Are you not aware that I speak of Polly Berridge? You are acquainted with her, and can bear witness to my description."

"Indeed," answered Mrs. Denton, "she is a good sensible girl, clean, tidy, and of agreeable person. I can recommend her to any lady wanting a maid."

"And I can recommend her to any gentleman wanting a wife."

"Do you fully mean your words?"

"Without abatement," he answered courageously. "I have more than once seen the father, Berridge, an honest man—"

"Yes, Berridge is an honest man."

It was Mr. Paul Denton, who entering, overheard the last words, and according to wont, took them up.

"He is honest, and honesty is the best policy; therefore he is a politician. See how virtue can be translated to the same sense as villainy, so that one would almost say they mean the same. Berridge, no doubt, is an honest man as men go."

" And how do they go, pray ? " asked his friend.

" Not all fours, but with a limp. Berridge is an honest man, and Polly, his daughter, is —what, Gray? a charming girl ? "

This was said so archly that Gray constrained himself to answer seriously, and with valiant stress—

" Very charming."

" Quoth Don Fernando, the Spaniard, concerning Donna Isabella the Spaniardess. When I called the other day, Martha, no less than three gallants waited on her."

" Why not four ? " said Mr. Gray.

" Making me the fourth ? "

" Nay, the first, if you like."

" Dare I advance any pretensions after the rebuff that I received? Martha, this same Polly Berridge, whom I remember as a quiet modest girl with but little to say for herself—But you, Gray, have forestalled me in my story."

" No," said Mr. Gray ; " you have the market to yourself."

" You were about it."

" By no means."

" Come, how many have you made merry with it already?"

" Not one."

" Then you have never a friend to rejoice with over the piece that you have found."

" I hope I have, if I had need."

" You hope you have, having no need. Since you have been so neglectful of this little friendly office, I might keep it secret, if it were not for those two youngsters; but you could as well gag a north-east wind on a mountain as a full mouth in an empty head. Well, this charming girl, Martha, was good enough to inform me in exchange for some of my smallest compliments that if I were not an old gentleman, she should consider me very impertinent."

" Indeed?" said Mrs. Denton.

" A pretty choice between the irresponsible imbecility of age and the irrepressible impertinence of youth! Oh, her spirit has been daintily stalled, fed on flattery, corned with vain hopes to grow so unmanageable. You have heard of that foolish lad, Gray? Do you not find food there for suspicion?"

"No, Paul," returned Mrs. Denton, in her quietest manner, "I hope there was no ground for her reproof."

"I thank you for the hope. However, I have advised you, admonished Humphrey, warned Berridge, and now events may go their own way. Good-day to them if we must part ; I keep straight on."

There was a short pause, during which each might be thinking of what displeased him best, the common matter of our cogitations. At last Mrs. Denton said—

"You say, Paul, that you have warned Berridge. Of what, pray, have you warned him?"

"Of what but Humphrey's intimacy with his daughter?"

"Do you mean," she asked with severity, "that you accused my son of evil designs against her?"

Her brother-in-law felt it really too bad to have his good endeavours questioned in that way, but still replied—

"Not at all. I let him know that if he had designs they could not be good ; and if he had none, the same bad issue would drift along the current."

" The same thing," said Mrs. Denton, " evil deeds do not spring from good intentions."

" What I say might be said of any man that is a man and young, or of any old man that has a habit of folly."

"You were greatly to blame, Paul," said Mrs. Denton gravely, thrusting his crafty wisdom aside.

"And shall be more greatly blamed," he replied, with as much gall as he cared to disturb his digestion with. " In doubtful courses every action is blameworthy, but inaction most; and all take their share of blame except that which merits most; its Benjamin's portion is divided among its brethren."

"You are too self-sufficient, Paul; you give out the world dishonest and unclean, and to prove it you make it so. Why are you so ready to imagine evil in another, before he has any thought of it? By what right do you create wickedness and impute it to my son? What was foul was not his intention but your suspicion, not his action but your correction."

" Ha ! what next ? what next ? "

" This ; all that is wrong you have made wrong, and we look to you to right it."

" He who would benefit any one in spite of himself is the unluckiest fool in the world. Well, Martha, I wish that you may never regret it."

" I think not, Paul ; I have no doubt that Polly Berridge will make an excellent wife."

" What," said he, wholly upset, " are you ready to countenance them so ? "

" How else could I countenance them ? "

" Anyhow, rather," he answered recklessly, harassed, but promising to hold his ground ; when suddenly he retreated, muttering as he went, " but if a woman has her mind set, you can as well change her face." He had now opened the door. " To change her face is easy to that, and oftener done."

Which shaft having launched Parthianwise, in a moment he was on the other side of the door out of danger. Mr. Gray had watched the scene amused, though interested, and now came forward and said—

" Are you then resolved ? "

" Not to be unjust," she replied.

With that she rung the bell, and on a servant's appearance ordered him to request Polly's immediate presence.   Until when the two friends sat together, too thoughtful for much speech, each for the time making himself god of circumstances and ordering all things well.

CHAPTER XI.

At last the door opened, and not Polly, but Humphrey entered the room, his gloom becoming still more discontented when he found that it was not empty. However, he came heavily forward with a faint greeting of doubtful blessing, and heaped himself upon a distant chair. Mr. Gray looked significantly at Mrs. Denton, who rose and went to her son, and kissing him said—

"What is the matter with you, Humphrey?"

No answer.

"I have been thinking, my dear son, and find that I have been hasty, prejudiced, hard, cruel."

Still no answer, and vanquished pride began to mutiny in the motherly breast, but was at once overpowered.

"Nay, make your eyes less sullen, my dearest. If you do love Polly Berridge that is no reason why we should not love each other. What, no light yet!"

None, though his heart had started at his

love's name. A fresh struggle, another victory, and then the mother must kiss him again, and again say—

" Do you fear your mother will be a block on your happiness ? All shall be done to your desire. ' Will not you answer ? We will have an early wedding, anything that you wish." '

The elderly man was thinking what a godsend it was to be tenderly beloved ; and even the young one undisciplined was fain to kiss the hand that rested on him, though he withheld his eyes and answered under cloud—

"My wish is, mother, that nothing more be said of it."

" I cannot read you, Humphrey," said Mrs. Denton, perplexed and disheartened.

Rising, but still looking from her, he answered —

"Mother, take all that you have read as a foolish passage without context, not worth a second perusal. Notwithstanding, I thank you, and wish I could thank you better."

" Pooh," said Mr. Gray, coming up, " it is only a lovers' quarrel, a deadly half-hour's quarrel."

"You are mistaken," answered Humphrey, as he left them, "we are not on loving enough terms to quarrel."

The two remaining looked at one another at a loss what to think of it; but the direction of Mrs. Denton's thoughts was shown at last by her words.

"Has the fond girl rejected him? What are her dreams of? A better husband, a better match?"

"Ah," answered Mr. Gray's experience, "I have lived and seen so many misapprehensions that grew first to separation and then to regret. Before censuring anyone let us know how much blame lies against your brother. His interference was well meant but unhappily planned, and may have raised troubled thoughts in still minds. Or our youngster may call prudence indifference. How could he help it, being in love? The two look much of a colour, especially in the evening, though the one is a saint and the other—not so to lovers."

Mrs. Denton replied—

"I see that I have been altogether in the wrong, and since this is the day for yielding

I'll yield entirely. Without authority Paul went to the Berridges and laid an injunction; I will take it off with authority."

At this point Polly was announced, and Mr. Gray passed out, saluting each lady with a bow dating from times when courtesy made old backs supple. Mrs. Denton received the girl kindly, made her be seated, and explained that she had a piece of lace that was in want of repairs, which she produced.

"How beautiful!" cried Polly, with professional interest.

"Yes," answered the lady, "it is a fine old point lace. I intend it for my son's bride, if it please God to marry him in my lifetime. And, indeed, I believe that his wedding is near; you must have the lace ready, Polly."

She was curiously watching the girl's face, as she spoke, change from unconcern in which nothing of that morning appeared to interest and pale restraint. The silent storms within a narrow breast are more dreadful, more destructive than winter ocean's loudest upheaval; yet Polly answered quietly, though with a tinge of malice—

"I can't do it in less than three days, ma'am. May it wait so long?"

"Longer," said Mrs. Denton, smiling; "the wedding will not take place this week. Let us spread it out on the table to examine it better."

While they are so engaged Mrs. Denton continues to speak, still observing the effect of her utterances.

"My son talks of travelling this autumn."

"I hope he may have a fair voyage," said Polly, anything but cordially.

"Voyage? He does but cross the Channel."

"What a pity! He won't visit Fiji then?"

"O, dear no."

"Nor New Guinea?"

"Certainly not."

"Nor Dahomey?"

"Only the Continent," at last answered Mrs. Denton, in some surprise at the regions to which Polly would relegate her son.

"Do you say Continent, ma'am, or incontinent? I know little geography."

A wildly beating young heart had Polly!

"Continent, certainly," replied the lady.

" See, this is a bad rent. You weren't long
at school, I believe ? "

" No, ma'am."

" Yet you seem well taught."

Here Mrs. Denton ceased to examine the
lace, and sat down again beside the mender.

" Perhaps you have studied at home ? "

" Yes," answered Polly.

" And have had teachers no doubt ? "

" Yes."

" Am I wrong if I fancy that Humphrey
was one ? No ? "

Polly answered reluctantly—

" He has kindly lent me many books,
and offered more help than I would
accept."

" So had I thought," said the mother,
gently taking her by the hand ; " for now as
I listen, you seem, if it is not fanciful, to
have caught his very accent, modes of speech,
most peculiar tones. Your whole conduct—
forgive me, Polly, if I am mistaken—appears
so infected with his influence of phrase,
gesture, and conceit, such tricks as are only
noted by every mother, that to see and hear
you always would be to have a womanly copy

of him constantly by. Such as his sister
might have been if she had lived."

Polly turned away her head in shame-faced
vexation at learning how much of her was
not her own, and murmured—

"I can't say what tricks I might have
caught of him."

That could scarcely have been meant for
Mrs. Denton's ears, but nevertheless reached
them, and she replied, still retaining her hand
and anxiously scanning her face—

"Ah, Polly, what bitter over-ruling spirit
is that which possesses you and transforms the
simplest of things to darkness and subtlety?
What ails you?"

"Nothing, ma'am; I drank rue this morning for my health."   So answered Polly,
taking note chiefly of the carpet.

"Polly, you are speaking too darkly and
cunningly for a free undistempered mind.
Look at this delicate network and see how
easily it is damaged in handling. Then the
tiniest rent being started soon runs through
the piece, and with great pains is hardly
mended. Do not be perverse; what you
would have that is good to have, take easily,

not grudging, but thanking God. Look again at the work; see how prettily natural flowers are mixed with the artist's own quaint conceits; an old-fashioned, easy-tempered poem of fauns, and nymphs, and lambs, and piping shepherds, and summer weather always."

So Mrs. Denton did not wait for a response to her appeal, which Polly did not dare as yet altogether to understand, but left it to work, and passed easily into more general talk. At last a servant entered and announced the arrival of a visitor. Mrs. Denton had to quit the room, and Polly was left to combat alone with a legion of imaginations. First she would try to calm herself and think out the meaning of what she had heard; then she would not think at all—it would be so dangerous to think wrong; and having so resolved, thought the more. "Mrs. Denton fancies so and so; that we are not grateful to Mr. Humphrey for past kindness. How much she is mistaken! Our gratitude could kill us, it is so vehement, so incurable a disease. But how do I know that she was speaking of him at all? There are fifty things that she might mean. At all events she meant little, or she would have taken pains to speak plainly. Why am I so unquiet and feverish? It is the heat."

The agitated girl went to a window, opened it wide, and leant over the ledge.

"What is this marriage of Mr. Humphrey's? Is he so faithless to—"

Ah, how near to a false thought! She would think no more. And, indeed, she did her best to fulfil the word. Thinking not to think she paced the room, strove to be interested in the pictures that adorned the walls, opened a book, and read Humphrey's name in it. Alas, her thoughts used to carol like birds, not thinking of what they sung; but now they must be caged, poor things, and taught current tunes, and be hushed from their natural melody.

However, a diversion came in Mr. Paul Denton's coat, who entered the room, and at once fixed his keen eyes on her.

"Why, how came you here?" he asked abruptly.

"Mrs. Denton sent for me, sir."

"Then she is—humph—not so wise as she might have been when she was younger. I suppose I must not ask why she wanted you!"

"To speak to me about this lace, sir."

"Wedding stuff for all the world!"

Under his gaze she could not with all her efforts prevent a hot blush from overspreading her face. It was unreasonable, as she fully argued; for what was it to her but so much lace to mend? Mr. Denton also perceived her distress, and said—

"You have answered me, Polly."

"I, sir?"

"Again and again, Polly, most ingenuously. You will not show so much of your heart in your face after a few more years of folly. So it has gone so far, has it? Well, young woman, give me leave to say that it would have been better for Humphrey if he had never seen you. Doubtless I am very impertinent for so saying."

Polly was not less disturbed for that speech, but managed to say—

"I ought not to have answered you so, sir; I was perplexed."

"In such a case, Polly, the simple speak the truth, the more knowing lie. With which must you rank?"

" I would always speak the truth, though I be simple for it."

" So you maintain your censure? Well, I am not vindictive; I will not war upon the world because there's a hair under my shirt."

Humphrey had been restlessly ranging from room to room, and now, being aware that Mr. Gray and his mother had gone out, entered again, and faced another couple with him in mind. He was more surprised than before, but no more pleased.

His uncle called from the other end of the room—

" Don't leave us, Humphrey. 'Pon my soul, you're as shy as a school-girl that doesn't know her geography."

He approached, questioning them both with moody eyes.

" No need to make yourself such a scowling puppet; I have said a little of my thoughts, and shall waste my wisdom no further. The only pity is that I have no other nephew; then we might both make a choice."

" How, sir? " asked Humphrey, with no pretence of interest in the answer.

" Thus—I speak candidly—on one hand is this young woman, with all her effects and defects, and on the other, myself, with my present favour and final inheritance ; I should ask you to choose between them."

" Here, sir."

Perhaps his then appetite for contrariety made him readier with the response, which, if he had taken time to consider, might have appeared humiliating. But Mr. Denton was in no secret ; which did not hinder him from looking very wise as he answered—

" You know I have no choice, you simpleton. If I left all to almshouses you'd be sure some day to be a candidate. And you, young woman, I suppose you choose on that side, too ? Nay, don't hang your head ; this is the third time of asking, you know. It is also a case of true love with you ?"

But Polly was in no haste to reply ; seeing which Humphrey bent down to her ear and whispered with desperate earnestness—

" For heaven's sake answer, Polly ; answer once for all. I'll molest you no further. Speak, though you curse me."

Thus conjured, she let a gentle " Yes" peep through her lips. So faintly did it show that Humphrey could not believe it. Not so his uncle, who replied—

"Of course, and very prettily and blush-ingly said. But should you be surprised if this love of yours raised a nest of domestic plagues to harry both of you?"

Polly answered nothing, but took a quick, troubled glance at Humphrey. He apparently had not marked the words; he was still gazing at her, doubtful of his ears.

"Well," concluded the uncle, seeing the little impression that he made, "it is as use-less arguing with lovers as deaf politicians. But understand, for my reputation's sake, that I don't consent to these senseless pro-ceedings."

He took up his hat and left them. Hum-phrey was still in doubt.

"It is true, Polly, what I thought I heard, but durst not believe?"

"O, your uncle has warned us too well. How can I answer?"

"Then you confess that the warning fitted? Tush! he won't have a bottle of the oldest port fetched, but he drinks it. You'll gain him in a week; in a week he will be delighted to disagree with you, and there'll be such debates between common sense and uncommon sense—between a man and a woman—as never were. Answer me."

" How can I answer, having misjudged and abused you so ? "

" Never mind the past ; let it bury its own dead follies. What of this present, Polly ? "

" Say that you forgive me everything. And how much is that ? Base thoughts, hard words, cruel actions."

" Nothing, Polly, to the happiness you might afford me. Well, here is forgiveness for everything that needs it. And now ? "

She spoke as low as before ; but he was closer and heard better with a better hope.

" You heard true."

As Paul Denton was going out, not exactly in a fume—for smoke needs fire—but in the opinion that there would be little wisdom in the world when he was dead, he met his sister-in-law and Mr. Gray in the hall. He immediately began the attack.

" So you have accomplished this little Berridge affair, Martha ? "

" I hope to do so," she replied, in no way

touched; "but I must confess there is a strange hitch somewhere."

"Little fear that some one has removed it. They are together in the breakfast-room, only waiting for the day to be named."

Mrs. Denton walked towards the room to see if it were so, and was followed by the two gentlemen.

As soon as they entered, Humphrey led up the half-reluctant girl, saying—

"Receive my last gift, mother."

"Given for love, Polly?" asked Mrs. Denton, kissing her.

But Polly had no tongue, and Humphrey answered for her.

"Yes; thanks to my dear uncle."

"What!" thought the latter to himself, "may I have been deluded by my philosophy?"

While his sister turned to him, saying—

"My dear Paul, have we misunderstood you?"

"I see," he replied, "that there has been considerable misunderstanding somewhere."

"Let us forget it," she returned; and he, "I shall as soon as possible."

In truth, taking rapid stock of his position, he saw that it would only shake his credit to publish his losses, and he had better make capital of that windfall of generosity, and retrench.

Mr. Gray spoke at last, saying to him—

"So you have had a finger in the pie, after all."

"Not for myself; I believe in the ancient rhyme that apple pie makes you cry; but for these youthful digestions. I saw there was a hitch in the cookery, and know that nothing furthers that like a little masculine opposition."

Even Humphrey began to waver.

"Were you, indeed, uncle, more friendly than you seemed?"

"Shake hands, Humphrey, and leave questions for questionable matters. I wish you would begin to rail on me again, Polly."

"Why, sir?"

"That I might be excused for stopping your mouth; which I am tempted to do without an excuse."

It was a beautiful cheek that the little man touched, and he began to comfort himself with thinking that after all it would have come to pass, though Zadkiel had sworn the contrary. Besides, he liked opposition— or thought he did—it led to conversation—and had she not already sauced him in a most promising manner?

" Well," he said to Gray, as they departed together, " wise or otherwise, it's done. What do you think of it?"

" I think," he answered, laughing, " that you're a bit of a humbug, Denton."

" Hush, don't publish it, and I'll reserve what I think of you and the rest of mankind."

CHAPTER XII.

LET us look in upon our friends the Berridges this afternoon. We may enter boldly, for though it is five o'clock, there is nobody at home. Mrs. Berridge has gone to Nottingham market; Amos is delivering to customers; Polly—we know where she is.

Presently, however, we can hear Mike clattering along the garden-path, and forthwith he enters all at once. Finding no one in the kitchen, he begins to bawl—

"Mother! Polly! Hollo!"

Only silence answers and snubs him.

"Humph," is his conclusion; "nobody in, and the door unlocked. If 't had been me, whew! a fine leathering I'd ha' had, two minutes younger if I'd been."

He examines the cupboards, and, finding nothing more to his liking, cuts himself a huge slice of bread-and-butter, and sits down to eat it, with his feet on the bare brick, and with his free hand on the chair arm, drumming to the motion of his jaws.

" Hollo ! " cries someone, amid the din.

" Hollo ! " cries Mike, in answer, applying the soft pedal to his music. Looking round, he sees, at the half-open door, Mr. Chatterly, whom he knows, but does not esteem, longing to pitch into him, without knowing why.

" Mr. Berridge not in ? " asked Mr. Chatterly, entering.

Mike snaps a huge bite, and gruffly answers through it as well as he can—

" No."

" In soon ? "

" No."

Mr. Chatterly sits down at his ease, pushes his hat from his brow, lolls back on the chair, taps the floor with his cane, and makes himself at home, unconscious of Mike's wrathful eyes.

" Rather a nice place, this," he said at last, condescendingly, after surveying it from floor to roof.

Mike replied not. Woe to the bread-and-butter that day ! How ruthlessly he attacked it, cutting off even unto the remnant thereof. Plainly he was not in a conversational mood, and Mr. Chatterly had to be content with whistling. In a while he spied the piano in the corner, and straightway sitting down to it, began to strum.

"That's our Polly's piano!" cried Mike, fiercely glaring.

"Indeed! Well, our Polly's a jolly girl, isn't she?"

"What's that to you?" Mike would have answered, but it was choked up with bread.

"But her piano's a beastly bad tone."

Mike rose in ire, and with peril of life bolting a tremendous mouthful, growled—

"Well, you let it alone, then! Who asked you to touch it? Come, now!"

With a light contemptuous look, Chatterly struck another chord, and began to sing to it; but before "Polly, she's so jolly," was half out of his mouth, he was swept clean off the stool on to his back. Boiling with rage to be so handled by the factory lad, who still stood glowering over him with clenched fists, he started to his feet, prepared for battle. The combatants—the elegant, well-made young man and the raw, bony youth—faced each other for the onset, and now—. But hark, the door opens; and, lo, who but Humphrey, bearing his love on his arm, and his happiness on his face. Berridge follows, clad in more sober joy. Chatterly, with a laugh, thrusts his hands into his pockets, and, nodding to each, resumes his ordinary careless demeanour. Mike, less skilful in the face, stands as he feels, frowning injury.

"Why, what is the matter, Mike?" said Polly, detecting disturbance on the instant.

"What does he want banging your piano?" he replied gruffly.

Polly tried to laugh his humour down.

"Why, Mike, that's the fashionable style; twenty-five bangs, and then a little cheep."

But Mike was not to be mollified.

"Let him try, that's all."

Chatterly did not reply to the grim challenge, for he was talking to Berridge about apples. Perhaps he saw something displeasing in Humphrey's joyous face, and in Polly's arm that he still retained. At any rate, after giving his order, he departed less self-content.

Humphrey had now leisure to turn to Mike and say—

"Give me your hand, Mike; we are brothers now."

" Eh, what ? " cried Mike, astonished, but not withholding his hand. "My brother? Are you sure of it ? "

" Quite sure."

" Why, then—"

But the question was hard to frame, and Mike stopped short.

" Out with it," said Humphrey.

" Why, who's your father ? " he blurted out; and how they all laughed !

" Good, good," cried Humphrey, holding his sides.

" Well, your mother, then ? "

" Stupid Mike," said Polly, blushing and laughing equally.

" Well, then, who's my mother ? " he persisted.

" The Lord help thee, lad," said old Amos.

" Well, my father, if you like," said the bewildered lad, conscious of stupidity, and labouring to get out, like one lost in a wood.

At last, when they had laughed enough, Polly went up to him, and, abashed to hear her own voice, much more to be heard, whispered something in his ear.

" Oh ! " said the boy, with a bad attempt

at a whisper, "but you don't like him, do you?"

"Hush," she answered. "Yes, I do."

"But you said, you know—"

Kiss him, Polly, and block his mouth with your hand; and then, glancing timidly round at Humphrey, whisper—

"I will not say how much, for he is listening."

Before Mike can cause more confusion, for which he is ready enough, in comes Mrs. Berridge and her basket

"Why, Mr. Humphrey," she said, "how do you do, sir? But I needn't ask; you're looking uncommonly well. Bless me, what's the matter with you all, smiling, and nodding, and looking? Has somebody had a fortune left? As you stand, you look as like a wedding-party in a picture as might be. I remember when Amos—"

"Wedding-party!" yelled Mike, with delight. "Hooray! hoohoohoo;" finishing with a regular ogre's laugh, that came out like a flood, every sluice open.

"Bless the lad," said Mrs. Berridge; "what's he hoohooing at now?"

" In fact, Mrs. Berridge," said Humphrey, " I am looking to see a wedding-party of my own shortly."

" I'm glad to hear it, sir. Every young man ought to marry; and should, too, if I was his mother. And who's the lady, sir, if I may ask ? "

Humphrey made bold to kiss her on each apple-red cheek.

" For shame, Mr. Humphrey," she said, laughing, " before my husband here ! And you a married man, too, or as good as one, to take your word."

" Tell mother who the lady is, Polly," said the father.

" Yes, tell, Polly," said Humphrey.

" Tell, Polly," repeated Mike.

Mrs. Berridge begins to rub her eyes, crying : " Why, you don't mean to say ?— What am I thinking of ?—Mercy on my eyes !—Mr. Humphrey—Amos—Polly—what is it ? Lad, you'll break that chair-back, lolling on it that way. Sit up ! "

" Come, Polly," said Humphrey, putting his arm round her, and bending over to encourage her, " say."

Drooping her head, like a pretty red rose-bud, Polly tried to be calm, as she replied—

" You can tell it best, Humphrey."

" Ah ! what ? " said the mother, kissing her heartily. " Well, child, you needn't think I'm blind; I've two good eyes yet without spectacles. Who in the world would have thought it ? Bless you, my darling; you always were my favourite, you know."

" Next to Mike," said Polly, laughing.

" 'Sh, 'sh, or I shall never manage him no-ways. Women always do like their lads best, Polly, and so will you. Well, sir, I hope you'll be as happy as you deserve. Polly has good principles; and if she knows nothing about cooking, all I can say is, it isn't my fault. But I doubt you'll be wanting her to sing all day. Well, singing's all very well, and so's the piano, of an evening, but a good pudding's good any time o' day."

" I say, Mr. Humphrey ? " shouted Mike.

" What now, Mike ? "

" Hahaha. Father ! "

" Ay, lad ? "

" Hohohoho. Mother ! "

" What possesses the lad ? You'll choke to

death some day, and a fine funeral you'll make with your hoohoohoo."

"I say, Poll?"

"Yes, Mike!"

"Haw-haw-hee-hee-hoho-hooo—I say—ho-ho—I say, you won't—hoho—won't—hoohoo—sing 'Old Robin Gray' any more, lass! Ho-ho-hee-hee-ho-ha-hoo. Came a courting me—Oh, dear!—Old Robin—hoohoo—O my sides!—Old—heehee—Old—Where's my tea? I'm getting a reg'lar bacca-pipe!"

HOME AGAIN.

———

CHAPTER I.

ABOUT twenty years ago, in my young days, I was on a ramble through the wilds of upper Northumberland. And one night I happened to stop at a solitary hamlet, whose ancient quietude so won me, that I resolved to rest my weary ancles there for a day or two. So the next morning after the tea and eggs of my good cottager—for there was no inn in the place—I loitered out in the sun ever in a mind to sit, if I found a seat to my mind ; until I came to a church no bigger than any barn.

There I sat down on the low broken wall, and suffered my half-closed eyes to wander idly from under my hat over the building's rude mossy stones and the long grass, that had buried alike the graves and their memorials, leaving no work for Time to do.

But presently the sexton came shuffling along importantly to open the gate. After a while a clergyman appeared, looking no funeral. And then two carriages drove up, ancient vehicles of unknown name, such as still linger with other old fashions in remote country places, drawn by rough-coated cart-bred horses. Out of these stepped three gentlemen and as many ladies of no mean appearance.

I soon understood, more from their bearing than equipment, that I beheld a wedding-party; and more with their bearing than equipment was so much taken, that after witnessing the ceremony (which appeared to the two brides and their grooms, to the old clergyman, to the bridesmaid and best man, to the old sexton and myself, the sole spectators, to be of some solemnity), and after watching them out and away, until the farthest dust had settled behind their wheels, I still kept thinking of them. And still from whatever subject they started, I whistled my thoughts back to them, until I repaired again to my lodgings, and had to call my meditations home to dinner.

In the evening as I walked out again, I chanced to meet the clergyman. He kindly returned my dubious respectful salutation, and drew me on to talk with increasing freedom of this and that, his quiet village, a quaint cottage, yonder ancient farmstead, of the little church, and finally of the wedding.

"I do not wonder," said he, "at your curiosity, for indeed there is something extraordinary, both in those persons and their circumstances."

I ventured to press him a little ; and after a pause and a feeble putting-off that did not mean refusal, he courteously invited me into the spacious stone-built parsonage hard by, where he lived alone with an old servant.

After I had declined wine, and accepted tea, observed the antiquity of his house, and especially some curious carving on the staircase, and when I had finished admiring the garden and his housekeeper's cake, for which she was much celebrated in those parts, I began to remind him of my former enquiries. Without much delay he hemmed to clear a somewhat broken voice ; and then premising that he had received the confidence of most

N

of the parties concerned, and could therefore speak as it were *ex cathedra*, began a tale which he did not conclude before eleven o'clock, a monstrously late hour, as with many shamefaced excuses he confessed.

Whether it was from the intrinsic merits of the story, or from the interested face and simple kindly language of the narrator, it took great hold of me ; and many a time have I sat down after dinner in this arm-chair purposing to record the whole, but have hitherto been frustrated by the stubborn force of inactivity and an easy untroubled disposition that leaves me free to sleep.

However, now that I have begun, I hope to make an end of it. Let me only add, that for the truth of the matter, I would pledge and pawn my wife and her best gown. As to the style, I am but an unlearned man, therefore I would say, if you have not here words enough and good enough, you may buy all Johnson's Dictionary for a shilling and suit yourselves.

CHAPTER II.

He of the bridegrooms that most impressed me, was Geoffrey Cantrell by name; the more open face, his friend Roger Bonifant. They had equally been born to large fortune, high position, good name, and an uncommon friendship; had equally squandered all but the last in a common enough prodigality.

Then Mr. Cantrell's sister, Constant, a young lady of high principles and firm resolution, persuaded her brother at last to leave his folly and dissipation, his evil acquaintance and bad reputation, and with them three parts of his despair, in London, and to retire with the scanty remains of his wealth to a solitary house in the country.

Thither she accompanied him, thinking it nothing to sacrifice to him her friendships, pleasures, and occupations; and there she tended him and entertained him, busying herself only about him, until by degrees he gained composure if not cheerfulness.

He would fain have had Mr. Bonifant's com-

pany there, scarcely heeding even his sister's
entreaty against it, but was disappointed by
that gentleman's unexpected and obstinate
refusal. For Miss Cantrell had ventured to
speak privately to him, and had put him upon
his honour to decline the invitation.

She had all along put the weight of her
brother's excesses upon him, and had done all
in her power to break their connection; with
no success but in raising bitter jealousy
between herself and him. Do not think that
she had other motives; for doubtless she was
a dame both to reject another's vain fancies
and to repress them in her own heart.

Meminy Lodge, to which Mr. and Miss
Cantrell retreated, is six miles from Purley,
the hamlet which I have already mentioned,
and fifteen from Tattleby, the nearest market
town and railway station. It is an old stone
building of rude architecture and ample size,
bare to every wind; such as only troops of
merry inmates could enliven.

In front was a rough lawn, overshadowed
by a great sycamore, the only tree around,
and diversified by a few beds of the hardier
flowers, which Miss Cantrell caused her

brother to set out. Their household was composed of Jacob, the old man of all work, old Hannah, the housekeeper, a person of some consequence, and a stout, blowzy square-shouldered country wench.

The two former had been in the service of the late occupier of the house, and, boasting an attachment of generations to his family, " Back to feyther?" as they mumbled, " ay, an' feyther's feyther, an' feyther to that ; an' who knows how fur back, who knows ?" were inclined to regard our newcomers as inter-lopers.

In this retreat the brother and sister passed a year, Geoffrey employing himself in reading, walking, fishing, and other country pursuits, while Constant's sole occupation was Geoffrey. Meantime they received no news of Mr. Boni-fant, beyond learning from Lady Emily Hoton, Constant's faithful correspondent, that he was seen no more in town.

At the end of that time Geoffrey and Constant were walking together one day, and the sister was endeavouring to amuse the brother's dejection with all her merriest volu-bility. Making herself content with his short and unready, though affectionate, responses, she was talking gaily now of news from Lady Emily and the papers ; now of some book that he was reading ; or plucking the wild flowers that they trod on, she told him their names, properties, and traditions, or if they were unknown, embellished them as much as their beauty with daintily-tinted fancies and conceits.

So they were engaged, when on descending an abrupt hollow some miles from home, they suddenly came upon a man lying on the grass. At their approach he started up like one caught. It was Roger Bonifant.

Geoffrey stood dumb with surprise. Constant stepping forward in heedlessness or confusion, stumbled over a stone, and would have been flung headlong down the bank had not her brother just caught her by her dress. With the shock and the fright, she fainted away. The two young men, with no greeting but a look, laid her on the bank, and not knowing what else to do, began to fan her with their hats. At last she opened her eyes, sat up, and with a blanched smile, assured them that she had recovered.

Then the two friends found a few words to express their joy at the meeting. Even Constant seemed satisfied with her brother's happiness; and when Roger admitted in answer to repeated questions that for a year back he had been living at Purley or in the neighbourhood, constantly avoiding their encounter, she might have been taken to be greatly moved, could it not have been fairly put down to her previous faintness.

Not at all satisfied, Geoffrey began to question him further; but with a light look towards Miss Cantrell, he answered jestingly that a great aunt of his, to whose property he was greatly attached, and from whom he expected more than perhaps he should receive, had enjoined on him, as he valued her white wig, to avoid his friend's corrupting fellowship.

Geoffrey, still less satisfied, began with—

" But yet—"

" Stay," interrupted Roger, " won't it be best for Miss Cantrell to return home as soon as possible ? "

" Right," answered Geoffrey ; " but you will return with us, Roger, in spite of your great aunt and great expectations ? "

Roger closely watched, could have been seen to half turn towards Miss Cantrell, but as she made no sign, seeming to see nothing with her down-cast eyes, he assented, and they started together. The two friends, as you may suppose, had much to say to one another by the way; while, Constant, too, leaning on her brother's arm, at times put in a word. So that Roger, thinking he saw in her a friendlier mood, ventured now and then to address himself directly to her, a thing which he had not done for years; and she gave him no visible rebuff. So they reached Meminy Lodge in the best agreement.

You may guess whether that evening passed pleasantly; for Mr. Bonifant had been esteemed the merriest brain in London as long as his purse laughed at his jokes; then Geoffrey's wit, if more solid, was by no means wooden; finally Miss Cantrell, being woman —what more need I say?—was not speechless, provided she had anything important to deliver.

CHAPTER III.

THE next morning Roger rose early with
great cheerfulness, no doubt reflecting on the
likelihood of happier circumstances to his
intercourse with his friend. After a stroll in
that best, that maidenhood of the day—when
the sun has courted and kissed, not yet
wedded and embraced her—he returned to the
house to be greeted heartily by Geoffrey and
received by Miss Cantrell with the utmost
politeness. With the extremest courtesy he
was also invited to take his seat at the break-
fast-table. What is there more to say? He
preferred sugar to his coffee, and also cream,
I thank you. The trout was of her brother's
catching. Indeed? Mr. Bonifant had not
lately seen a finer fish. He would take an
egg with proper thanks. Nothing passed at
table but that, and that was all very proper.

Have you on some treacherous day felt
thunder in the air, seeing and hearing
nothing? Have you understood aversion
beneath all the forms of courtesy and

propriety ? It was apparent that Miss Cantrell's disapprobation had been asleep last evening, not dead, and with the morning it had awoke again. Nevertheless Roger and his friend walked to Purley that day and returned with what they could carry of his luggage; and doing the same on following days, soon permanently established him and his effects at Meminy Lodge.

There is no temptation to linger among thorns. You will understand how antipathy, veiled at first like a decorous obscenity, was more and more revealed as daily contact wore off its thin cloak; how Constant showed herself cold, suspicious, bitter; how Geoffrey grew anxious, discontented, gloomy; and Roger capricious, sarcastic, edged—forcing ill-timed merriment, affecting to regret his former jovialities, delighting to rouse Miss Cantrell's jealousy.

You shall have an example. At the end of a month Geoffrey and Roger were seated one day in the garden arbour, when Constant unwittingly entered. Seeing the two young men, she stepped back saying, with much expression of regret—

"I beg your pardon, Mr. Bonifant; I assure you, I was not aware of your presence."

"No apology needed, Miss Cantrell," replied Roger in a quiet, careless tone; "we are engaged in no talk at present that would disgrace any lady's ear."

"The accusation and defence seem to proceed from the same mouth," she rejoined coldly, erectly.

"Nay," he retorted; "heaven forbid my dulness reduce you to declare all your meanings plainly."

"Sir, I must not deny what you insist on so much," she proudly answered, and left them.

Roger looked at Geoffrey with something like indignation in his placable eyes. Geoffrey began to plead uneasily—

"Roger, don't think harshly of my sister, poor girl. She is the only thing of mine that good can be said of; my one good quality that saves me. You know what this mood of hers springs from. She holds me, forsooth, to be by nature the best of brothers; and whatever errors, shortcomings, follies, sins, and madnesses I may have shown, she lays upon your broad shoulders."

" Returned," quoth Roger," to their proper ass with proper thanks. I have as many of my own as I can bear, and have no sister to transfer them."

" I had sometimes wished," said Geoffrey, " that you could share mine."

" Thanks," replied his friend ; " I do not deny her goodness, even her tremendous goodness ; but you must pardon my declining."

" Do not unvalue her, Roger," cried Geoffrey.

" I do not," said he ; " I do not value her at all. The scornful girl would despise being a moment in my thoughts."

" Not scornful," said the brother, " but prejudiced."

" Then scornful only to me," his friend made return.

" Roger, no one can relate her goodness."

" For no one durst," muttered Roger underbreath ; and Geoffrey continued, unheeding it—

" You know how I wasted my youth—"

" And I mine."

" And fortunes—"

" And I mine."

" In the most prodigal dissipation ?"

" In which I was your equal and very good comrade, who found your society far more entertaining then than now."

" You know," Geoffrey went on, taking firm hold of his voice, " you know how gently, how wisely, how constantly (up to her own sweet name), how lovingly, how—in short, how sisterly she redeemed me, buying me back with herself?"

" And what of me ?" cried Roger rising in his impatience. " No doubt she would scorn to redeem me, the proud woman, even if I would let her ; but where is our inequality ? I threw my money away as recklessly as you, not more ; I wasted my prime as riotously as you, not more ; I have reaped regrets as abundantly as you, not more. And why should she persecute me ? Why hold hourly *auto-da-fés*, and lash me, and goad me, and roast me, benefiting neither soul nor body, but only to satisfy her most religious zeal ? Why not hand me over to Calcraft and the secular arm at once, and have done with me?"

"What can I say, Roger? You know the truth; she thinks we have not been a good influence to one another."

"Or rather she only cares to think that I have been an evil influence to you. No doubt I have helped you, and you me; a pair of very helpful scapegraces, as well-matched as any two pigeons that were ever plucked."

"A sister's partiality," pleaded her brother.

"Certainly, if you do not talk of justice!"

"I might as well talk of John o' Groats. But what can I do? She dreads my excuses; and whatever I say only fixes her the firmer."

"Constant in all," cried Roger. "I tell you what, Geoffrey, with your leave, she is the proudest, stiffest-necked woman from here to London. Had I more years than you? Larger experience? Different circumstances? Will she allow me a jot more brains, as she might? or anything more except more blame? What reason has she but a sisters's reason?"

"And that is enough for her," answered Geoffrey with emotion. "You must forgive her, Roger. God bless her."

" No doubt He will," said Roger a little
more soberly; and then began again : " In
fact, my friend, Miss Constant's object is to
drive me away from you, but in that she shall
not succeed; I pledge myself to it; I will be
as obstinate as herself.   Prepare yourself for
what you are about to hear; I prolong my
visit until she presses me to stay."

" I pity you," quoth Geoffrey, "as much
as myself.   One of us must die by this
affliction."

" Well, I am the stronger, thank heaven."

" By no means."

" Nothing surer."

" Except Turkish bonds."

" I can fling you."

" Try."

" Agreed."

So gladly throwing off their mental
difficulties and their coats, the two friends
engaged in bodily wrestle ; and when at last
they had abandoned the fruitless and too
equal struggle they were talking earnestly of
the Cumberland and Cornish styles.

However, Geoffrey took the opportunity to
speak to his sister one day, when she had

given more than usual expression to her tender affection for him.

"I wish that Roger had been our brother, Constant."

"A sufficiently graceless wish," she replied. "And why?"

"That you might have been willing to forgive and forget the faults that he has shared with me, and to influence him for his improvement."

"You wish me a tedious, heavy task on hand, Geoffrey. But, perhaps you are only wishing me a long life."

"I do not think Roger so unimpressible," said he.

"Nor I," said she, "to certain impressions."

"Ah, you are too bitter to him, Constant."

"Nay, my dear brother, it is he who is too bitter to me; and if the draught makes my mouth wry, am I to blame?"

"I know your antipathy," he replied; "a thing hard to reason against; but if you cannot cure it, cannot you cover it, even for hospitality's sake?"

"I never thought of hospitality," she said. Mr. Bonifant is so much at home here."

"A rather uncomfortable home, I fear," Geoffrey answered somewhat gloomily.

"Is he not quite free to change it?" asked Constant mildly cruel; and then returning a little as she saw her brother's countenance change, "Nay, do not be angry with me, my dear Geoffrey."

"I could not, Constant, even if I had the desire and a good cause. If for my benefit you have left your friends and changed your life, it would be too much to require you, for my humour, to alter your opinions and quit your natural sentiments."

"Listen, Geoffrey," she said more seriously, "and do not think me hard or willing to reckon back; I would recall nothing but reconciliation; yet if I could not approve of your former uncongenial ways, how can I of your companions in them? I cannot approve of Mr. Bonifant."

"Rather say this, my sister, and it will be more equal if not juster: 'If I can excuse a worthless brother, why not his not more guilty friend?'"

She only shook her head.

"Shall I never convince you," he proceeded

with loving, self-remembering sadness, "that I am your unworthy brother, and poor Roger my very fit and equal associate?"

"You shall convince me of nothing as to yourself, my dearest Geoffrey," she rejoined with an unanswerable caress, "but what I can prove for myself; for you are the most audacious, false witness against yourself, the veriest slanderer and tattler that I ever heard. See! the sun is dipping behind the Cheviot Hills; do you not offer me your company for stroll?"

CHAPTER IV.

A FEW days after this Constant received a letter from Lady Emily, announcing that she was about to visit the Lakes and entreating her friend to repair thither to her that they might for a time renew their happy familiarity. To which Geoffrey gave so strenuous a support, that at last his sister reluctantly consented to leave him for the utmost of four days. On hearing this Roger gave out that, strangely enough, he also had resolved to set out on a fishing ramble that very day for the same length of time. To this Constant listened with all the civility she could, glad at least to have him out of the house during her own absence.

A carriage was ordered from Tattleby to convey the lady to the railway station there; dresses that had been abandoned for rough country fashions were put in order; and many an injunction was laid upon old Hannah, as if Geoffrey was to be more cared for in her absence than presence. Meanwhile, Roger gave no sign and made no preparation for his promised excursion, which, indeed, Geoffrey merely regarded as another of the covert sarcasms that he heard pass between his sister and his friend too often for him to trouble himself to understand them.

Nevertheless, on the morning of Constant's departure, as Geoffrey was fastening her trunk down in the hall, Roger appeared before him, rod in hand, decked out in one of those costumes that make our tourists more wonderful sights abroad than any which they travel to behold.

" What ! " cried his friend, " do you mean to accomplish this fishing trip of yours ? "

" Did I not say so a week ago?" he replied.

" True," said the other; " but if it had been a century ago, you would have been as likely to stick to it."

" We cannot all be constant," said Roger innocently.

But Geoffrey, elastically bouncing off from that hard subject, raised himself from over the box and sat on it, saying—

" However, I am glad of it; for to tell you the truth—"

" Which I could as well tell you," cried Roger.

" Boredom, I find, is a dweller in the fields as well as in the cities."

" That last yawn of mine," quoth Roger, returning it full, " nearly cracked my jaw."

" Then you will talk the less."

" Nay, I shall be unable to stop talking."

" Would to mercy that you had broken it."

" Then it would have been like a broken dam, flooding you with broken English! But your weariness, at least, is strange, friend Geoffrey ; for, speaking impartially, I esteem my society the best possible ; at any rate, it is the only one that I could not dispense with."

" For you could find no one to dispense it to. Heigho, this is a dull house of ours ! "

" As melancholy as a winter ferry," assented Roger.

" And it will be thrice duller now that Constant leaves it. She is the only sauce and season of the insipid dish."

" Ay," said Roger ; " curry and cayenne. My yawning remarks were only for you, my friend ; your sister never bores me. She pierces me, transfixes me at a thrust."

"I am told that pig-sticking is very good sport," said Geoffrey.

"Very poor for the animal," said Roger. "Hush, the proctor!" he called out, not too low, as he caught sight of Constant descending the stairs.

Perhaps she heard it; perhaps with a good-natured fellow's spite he intended her to hear it. At any rate, she appeared with a slight unusual flush on her cheeks, and none the less lovely, as some might have thought, had they been there; but Roger did not look at her.

"Are you ready to start, Mr. Bonifant?" she enquired.

"No," he replied, somewhat doggedly for so good-humoured a man; "I have not decided yet on going at all."

"Very well," she answered composedly; "Jacob will bring your knapsack up, when you bid him."

"My knapsack?" he said with surprise, looking up for once. "I have none."

She answered—

"I believe one has been found for you somewhere among Geoffrey's things."

At that moment Jacob entered, bearing the knapsack in question.

"Oh," said Roger, almost peevishly, "I cannot be troubled with it. I would as soon be a snail, and carry my house."

"Indeed, you will find it necessary," reasoned Constant, coldly polite, "on these wild hills, where you will find none of the conveniences, I say nothing of luxuries, to which you are accustomed."

"You are referring to times, Miss Cantrell, when I was richer than I am now?" was Roger's question, which Miss Cantrell could not have heard, so quietly was it spoken, for she continued impassively—

"Really you cannot go without one. This is not Bond Street, Mr. Bonifant."

"For nothing binds me here," he responded with a slash that cut the colloquy clean in two. Nothing remaining to be said, he took the knapsack from Jacob, and with much weighing of it in his hand and much underbreath grunting and pshawing, got it nevertheless on his shoulders, in spite of his words. Then, slowly picking up his rod, and slowly taking down his hat, he turned and said, "Farewell,

Geoffrey; I leave you to yourself. You will find it no better company than mine. Miss Cantrell, I wish you a very good morning."

"Good morning to you, Mr. Bonifant," was her correct response; while Geoffrey called from the doorway—

"A good day's fishing and good night's lodging, Roger."

Soon afterwards a wonderful hired vehicle, drawn by a wonderful hired animal from Tattleby, conveyed Miss Cantrell away, and Geoffrey was left alone.

CHAPTER V.

In the evening of the same day he was on the lawn, taking in as much of the gentle breeze, the flowers' scent, the birds' hushed cradle-babble, and all the setting day's unemulative beauty, as his heart, so long stuffed with folly and vanity, could receive. All at once he was aware of a lady in black, with a small travelling-bag in her hand, hastening across the grass towards the house, looking about all the while from window to window and from side to side, as if in some expectation or uncertainty. He approached in curiosity. She, perceiving him, hesitated, and then turned to meet him; a young woman in a dusty, disorderly dress, with a pale, girlish face and a timid but eager air.

"Sir," she asked, "can you tell me where my grandfather is?"

"Your grandfather?" he repeated, surprised.

"I mean Mr. Hartwell," she said, as if in sufficient explanation.

"I do not know the name," he replied. "But I am almost a stranger to these parts. Have you not made some mistake?"

But ere he had finished, she had turned away quickly, had gained the house, had entered the open door, followed as fast as was seemly by Geoffrey in much wonder, ready for much pity. Pursuing the sound of her footsteps through the stone-paved hall, he reached the kitchen door in time to see old Hannah stand up in doubtful expectancy before the trembling girl, and to hear the repeated question—

"Hannah, where is my grandfather?"

"It is Miss Mercy," the beldame cried, with uplifted hands.

They fell on one another's neck, embracing their sorrow; while Geoffrey softly withdrew before the sight of the old face and the young face weeping together.

Ah me! is it not an ancient oft-proved sorrow to return home to what is home no more; renewing the mourning for an old loss; weeping young tears over an aged grief; performing fresh burial over the forgotten past; making resurrection of dead friends, even that they may die again, and be lamented again, and entombed again?

*   *   *   *   *

Geoffrey had sat an hour in the dark before Jacob appeared with candles, and began at once—

"Sir, sir, we's seen a sight this day to be thankful for, an' to be sorry for."

"Who is this young lady?" said Mr. Cantrell.

"Our young missis, the Lord be praised, noo th' oald master be dead, His will be done," he replied, ignoring his then wage-payer.

But we must abridge the old man's tale, with its ejaculations and confused wanderings, ever going abroad and not returning home till dark; and, for clearness, we will add other particulars only afterwards discovered.

Mr. Hartwell was the former owner and occupier of Meminy Lodge. Inheriting a mortgaged estate and an unencumbered generosity, his means had yearly become more straitened, until the younger Mr. Hartwell, his only child, was compelled to task himself with their restoration. Hoping to find in America the opening which he could not make in his own country, he emigrated thither with his motherless little daughter, Mercy. It would be no pleasant office to describe at large the manifold failures of an easy temperament, unused to application, always living on to-morrow, more willing to suffer than do, in the rough working world in which he now woke up bewildered. Enough that by the time Mercy touched womanhood, he was a broken man, who, after seeing fore-closing failure sell up the hopes that he had so heavily pawned, finally lost even serenity of spirit, his last possession. He died, and left his daughter to make her way back to England.

Thence no letter had been received for a year back, although Mercy had written thither, if not often (for misfortune is a hard word to be often spelling) at least sufficiently. However, this was a small surprise to them, for their changes of residence latterly had been frequent and great; and, besides, they knew that the old gentleman, being no ready writer, was never eager to set hand to paper.

Before starting homeward, the young lady sent her grandfather notice of what had happened ; again on the night of her touching England, she wrote apprising him of her arrival and of the hour that she should reach Tattleby on the following day. When, therefore, she arrived at that station, it was with much anxiety that she found no one there to receive her. She left her heavier luggage at the station, and, taking a small bag of necessaries in her hand, sought the principal inn of the little town for a conveyance. Their second carriage was already engaged, and on the point of starting with a lady travelling some miles further, but in the direction of Meminy Lodge ; who, being on the spot and hearing, gave up of her own accord a half share in its inconveniences.

Now it happened that Miss Hartwell only mentioned her grandfather's house, and not himself, during the few minutes at the inn; and being herself grown beyond recogniti n, thereby escaped news that must otherwise have been communicated, for Mr. Hartwell was a name well known for miles round. On the road, indeed, she made enquiries of the coachman, but he was a fresh man, he said, and a stranger to the country; the lady also was only a visitor from the south. Miss Hartwell alighted at the end of the short lane that led up to the house; the chaise drove on; and thus she ignorantly returned to her former home, and found her only guardian deceased, his possessions divided among unsatisfied creditors, his house in the hands of those who knew not even his name.

When Mr. Cantrell had heard all that Jacob had to say, it was agreed that the young lady should rest there that night under the house-keeper's protection; and that the next morning a look-out should be kept for the return of the chaise which had brought her up, so that she might find as quick a conveyance back as possible.

CHAPTER VI.

THE next day, while Geoffrey was eating his
breakfast, he learnt from Hannah that his
intruding guest was more composed in spirit,
but in body faint and unstrung, as well with
the fatigue of her long journey as with the
shock of her unexpected sorrows. As much
as he might, he pressed her, through the old
housekeeper, to remain a day longer for the
recruitment of her health; but it was reported back that she was firmly resolved on
departure.

But the clouds, whose distant artillery had
been heard since daybreak, as they mustered
their dark squadrons on the western horizon,
now came full on in one huge array, daunting
the heart of the solitary traveller, and the
cattle on the hills. The air grew thick and
dark. A short preluding spatter, and then
such a torrent of fire and water, as if it were
the last. There was no likelihood that a
hostler who cared anything for his beast or
himself, would bid either turn out of comfortable quarters.

Geoffrey spent most of the morning in loitering in and out of the different rooms that opened into the great hall, pacing them measuredly to and fro, and pausing at times to gaze through the doorway at the drenched landscape. If in any degree he lingered about in the curious hope of catching a glimpse of his guest, in case she left the housekeeper's little room, he was disappointed; therefore we hope that it was not so.

After a brief menacing lull towards noon, the storm came on again in the afternoon with all its reserves, amid a tremendous vehemence of thunder and lightning, hail and rain. So that Miss Hartwell, who was naturally of a nervous temperament, and then further inclined that way by her weak, unhopeful condition, was terrified to the last degree. Falling on the faithful housekeeper's neck, she hid her face in her bosom, sobbing and crying aloud. Hannah, after vainly doing her best to soothe the highly-wrought girl with rude caresses and simple encouragements, such as she had used to comfort her infancy, was fain in the end, after much hesitation, to despatch Jacob, begging for

Mr. Cantrell's assistance. He came readily, and found the girl strained against the old bosom, her hair in admirable disorder tossed over her face and shoulders, her fair arms extended round the withered neck, her eyes dark, her cheeks white, her lips all agony. After much persuasion and even injunction, given with that calm gentle firmness which so much imposes on weaker natures, he succeeded in inducing the young lady to cease her sobs, then to loosen her hold of the old woman, in a while to sit up with a countenance pale indeed and touchingly troubled, but dispossessed of terror; until finally with a timid abashment she could venture falteringly to excuse her fears. Yet dreading a relapse, Mr. Cantrell thought it well to continue his presence, and by degrees so occupied her with lively and entertaining talk, which he was well able to do, that she ceased to mark each flash of lightning save with a slight start. By five o'clock the storm had greatly abated, and through a breaking cloud the sun shone suddenly out with an almost mad glory, and heedless of the still pelting rain, poured out such a

P

torrent of splendour, as there had been before of water and hubbub.

Hannah now with aged bustle set about preparing Miss Mercy a cup of tea, from which she prophesied many good effects. Geoffrey was invited to take a share, and made no effort to decline, still using his tongue the while with so respectful a gentleness and so evident a desire to soothe and encourage his guest, that her fears were forgotten, her sorrows set aside if not put away, and she began to take a part so far as modestly to answer his willingly frequent questions, showing therein a natural vivacity oppressed by a not unnatural despondency.

Soon after Geoffrey had retired to eat his dinner in the solitary dining-room, the housekeeper conducted her charge to bed with motherly care. According to agreement her host despatched a note to Tattleby by the postman, ordering the "Peacock's" best chaise up to Meminy Lodge on the morrow.

CHAPTER VII.

THE following morning Hannah reported her patient as so ill, through yesterday's excitement working on a weakened frame, as to be quite unfit for travelling, and even unable to rise. So while the housekeeper busied herself with concocting herb teas and traditional simples, Geoffrey, having nothing better to do, as he said many times to himself, spent an hour in arranging a nosegay for the sick girl's room, which he sent up with a kind wish for her recovery.

In the middle of the day a battered chaise, which had endured the rebuffs of half a hundred years, arrived from Tattleby; but of necessity its driver was dismissed after due refreshment, and bidden return upon the morrow. Nevertheless, he had not long been gone, when Miss Mercy, who had apparently been roused by the sound of the departing wheels, came downstairs fully equipped for the journey; and to her nurse's surprise looked in at the kitchen-door.

"Pity huz, Miss Mercy!" she cried, raising her hands. "What is thee aboot?"

"Well, Hannah, what am I about?" said the young lady, with a would-be smile at the old woman's pathetic astonishment. "Did I not hear the chaise?"

"Shay! Did body iver hear?" said Hannah, addressing the ceiling. "What's thee talkin' o' shays wi' that wearifu' white face?"

"Hasn't it come?" Miss Mercy faintly insisted.

"Mayhap 'tis cum, mayhap 'tisna cum; anyhap intil no shay this day thoo gets," Hannah replied with dogged tenderness.

"But I must go, Hannah, I must; I cannot stay here," was the attempt at resistance.

"An' why no? Where'll thee find hands, barn, to sarve thee like these? An' whose lap'll thee hide intil, when's frighted wi' levin? When thoo goes, mind ye well, ah goes; an' that's not this day. Thoo needn't hae any fear o' introodin'; though I scena well hoo thoo could introod i' t' hoose 'at's thine by reet if not by meet, an's bin thy

fadder's an' granfadder's afoor thee time oot
o' coont. Hoosiver t' master, him 'at's
master like noo—I sayna he's a bad master,
considerin' he's o' t' wrang name, an' not
e'en o' t' country; an' t' young leddy, his
sister, she med be a hangel, for a' a body
could sweer. Awell, Master Cantrell, for
that's his name, as ah tell'd thee, he'll be fain
to hae thee bide as lang's need be, or thoo's
a mind. Sae much he tell'd me himsel. As
why sudna he? Nae better leddy an' nae
bonnier face, he'll see this sumwhile, ah
warraud; an' sae he were thinkin' yestreen,
as ah seed wi' a gleek."

"But Hannah, I cannot stay, it's impossible," reiterated the pale face, not so pale
as before.

"Cum back till thy bed, child; or any-
ways, thoo wilfu' body, cum thee oot o' t'
draught 'at's blowin' clean through thee an'
through thee. Theer, theer, sit thee doon,
an' be said. Aboot stayin' an' not stayin',
my bonny barn, an' unpossable, an' siklike,
it's unpossable thoo sud gae; for Bod Midgett's bin wi' t' black an' white shay, not t'
yeller an' red ane—that's bin bought years

agoo by oald Farmer Trudgett, when he married his dairymaid, t' blowzy trollop. But as ah were sayin', Bob Midgett druv up, an' t' master—that's t' new master I speaks o'—he bespak him himsel, sae bein's thoo's sae puirly, he sud cum again t' morn. An' gane is he this lang hoor or mair wi' many a slice o' beef an' many a mug o' yale the mair i'side him. He ay sets store by's belly, does Bob Midgett."

Just then Mr. Cantrell, hearing their voices as he passed the door, looked into the room, and expressed his surprise and concern at seeing Miss Hartwell downstairs in so weak a condition. She and the old housewife in unequal shares gave the explanation; for Mercy, though distressed at her situation, was too languid in body, as well as too considerate of her host's kindness, to give more than a short and feeble expression to her feelings. Mr. Cantrell excused himself; and then, as she still showed a disinclination to obey her nurse's recommitment to bed, said again—

"Well, Miss Hartwell, since the weather is so mild, let me carry you out on to the lawn the largest arm-chair I can find, and place it under the shadow of the great sycamore. There, if Hannah will provide wrappers, you may sleep more comfortably than anywhere. I promise that nothing shall disturb you."

That just hit the girl's sick and longing mood. So Geoffrey with great exertions carried from the dining-room an ancient oaken arm chair of huge size, assisted to seat her in it, placed a footstool under her feet; and when she had been enveloped carefully—too carefully she complained unheeded—in manifold rugs and cloaks, he respectfully withdrew with the housekeeper, and left her to herself. Left her to throw back her wrappings in gentle rebellion, to open her forehead to the young breeze, and breathe full of its gracious air; while she rested her eyes with quiet delight on all the familiar beauty around, then closed their lids only to feel it the more, until she fell asleep and dreamt of peace.

Geoffrey, chancing to pass within long view of her, saw that she slept. He softly drew near, and found something so admirable in the beautiful unrestraint of her slumber, that leaning against the old sycamore, he stood and held his breath and gazed into her face, like one taken in a vision which he fears to break. Miss Hartwell, when she awoke, found her lap and feet all bestrewn with flowers. But though Hannah soon returned to lead her back to the house, she asked no question as to who had placed them there. Therefore, the former, after staring dumbly a minute, began the interrogation herself.

"My certy, who 'll ha' bin doin' this?"

"I don't know, nursey; I have been asleep."

"'Tisna Jacob, ah reckon; h'aes too oald a pate to fash himsell wi' sic whimaleeries; it mun be nobbut t' master. Though who'd ha thowt it o' him, an' him sae dour, leastways sae mellicholy? for I winna say 'at he flytes an' bites at ane. Ah say sae, but marry, ah 've heerd him mesell talk awhiles for a' t' woorld like prent buiks," and so forth and so on; while Miss Mercy said nothing, and asked nothing, and doubtless thought nothing, and cared nothing.

CHAPTER VIII.

THE next morning Geoffrey again enquired after his guest.

"Ay, sir, she's better, she's better," Hannah replied shortly, grimly.

"But I suppose," he said doubtfully, "that another day's rest at least will be necessary for her complete recovery?"

"An' ah med ha' shupposed, sir, an' anybody med ha' shupposed," the old woman burst out, and then stopped.

Rightly judging from this that Miss Hartwell was now to take her leave, Geoffrey sent her a message by Hannah requesting in that case the favour of a short interview.

In fact there had been waged that morning by Mercy and the old servant as sharp a dispute as could be between them, when most of the words were on one side and most of the reason on the other. Hannah had been insisting with all the warmth of a crabbed, inveterate affection on accompanying her young mistress's departure. Blind to every

inconvenience in such a course, she chose to
impute refusal to an opinion of her useless-
ness, not to be resented without indignation.

"Well, well, Miss Mercy, sin thoo says sae,
dootless thoo thinks it is sae; but thoo 'll
find ah 'm not sae pithless as to sit a' day i'
t' chimney neuk like an oald wife, an' do nowt
but sneeze an' scold."

"But I don't say so, nursey," she answered; "you look quite young in your new
cap with pink strings. But you see I don't
know where I am going, nor what may happen
to me. Perhaps I shall find a situation as
governess or something of that kind, and live
in a family without a house of my own. And
then how could you live with me, dear?"

"Thee governessin', child? niver think it;
to be set on by hauf a score children, 'at 'ud
sarve thee like their rabbits an' birdies, an'
pu' thee to pieces in a twink. If 't were ane
barn noo, an' a girl, ah wouldna objeck sae
muckle; providin' they 'd treat ye becomin'
as a Hartwell-born, an' nane can say nay.
An' while thoo's i' t' parlour, why suldna ah
be i' t' kitchen? Theer's a many 'd be glad
—oald as ah be, an' crippled as ah be, an'

fizzenless an' thriftless as dootless ah be,—
theer's a many 'd be fain to hae a honest,
decent, sponsible sool i' t' hoose to shuperveese.
Theer's them as pays for victuals, 'at little
ken intil whose chaps they goes ; an' theer's
them as buys coals, 'at they ne'er sees the
burnin' o'. Shamefu', shamefu's t' waste ah
've seen an' heerd tell o'."

Mercy made no difficulty of assenting to an
arrangement which would doubtless prove
impracticable, but the strife was reopened,
when Hannah began to discover that she still
could not be allowed to set off straightway
with her mistress. In the end, however, she
was reduced to a grudging silence partly by
the necessity of attending to her duties, partly
by Mercy's caresses and promises to continue
writing to her, to do nothing without her
knowledge, and—most comforting of all — to
ask her advice before every step taken, with
no undertaking, however, to follow the same.

A few minutes after the housekeeper had
left with Mr Cantrell's message, Miss Hartwell came. It seemed that she was eager to
be gone ; for she was already dressed for
travelling, though the morning was yet but

little advanced. Her host led her out of the gloomy house into the garden, where they conversed, walking to and fro. A few ordinary words having passed, he began to say, as if with some hesitation—

"You may think it a liberty in a stranger, Miss Hartwell, to speak as I am about to do."

As he paused here, she said in a low voice, that she had no right to call him anything but what he had called himself, a stranger; but that his kindness had at least earned him the right, if he would, to speak with the freedom of a friend.

"You permit me to speak as a friend?" he asked.

She would be grateful to him for so doing.

"Shall I exceed a friend's license in conjecturing that you have but few friends in this part of the world?"

"Scarcely any," she said.

"Few, perhaps, anywhere?"

"Very few."

"Forgive me if I ask, whether you have any whom you can trust for everything?"

"I think not."

"And none of your kindred are left?"

"None," she murmured, drooping still her head until her hair fell from her shoulders all around her face, hiding what passed under it.

Geoffrey stopped a little in his cruel inquisition, and then proceeded.

"I do not wish to be impertinent. You let me speak like a busy friend?"

No audible reply was given, but he still went on carefully carelessly—

"From what Jacob and Hannah have let me know of their own accord, I must gather that like my own means, yours are but slight."

"It is so," came from under the golden veil.

Another pause ; and then—

"May I ask if you have any plans?"

"None as yet," she answered tremulously ; "the shock has been so great."

"You do not forbid me to be interested in them?"

"I cannot."

Then Geoffrey concluded—

"My follies and imprudences have taken

from me the right to give counsel ; but I have a sister older than yourself, and therefore, doubtless, in some things of more experience. Though her fortunes are gone with mine, she still possesses as many friends as I have lost, and a kind and gracious heart to boot. I dare not begin to praise her. If you need advice or any kind of assistance—it is not presumptuous to say so !—you will find her disposed to afford whatever is in her power."

A few scattered words came up ; that she thanked him, that she dared not trouble him further, and so on ; which Geoffrey rebutted with growing eagerness, until her undetermined resistance was overcome, and it was agreed that she should remain at Tattleby until Constant's return enabled them to consult together on her future courses. That concluded, Geoffrey led off into general talk, in which the lady, in view, I suppose, of their approaching separation, allowed herself more freedom than she had hitherto used. So they continued talking mostly cheerfully in spite of care, sometimes walking in the sunshine, sometimes resting under the sycamore's shade.

At noon Hannah came out to call her young

lady to luncheon ; who, on learning the hour, wondered a little that the chaise had not yet returned. However, she went in, accompanied by Geoffrey ; and both together sat down with the old housekeeper and partook of the refreshment. It was allowed, for they were so soon to part.

Still the afternoon advanced, and still no chaise appeared ; while Miss Hartwell's anxiety grew so visible, that for lack of other comfort Mr. Cantrell offered to walk along the road and see it if was anywhere in sight. He climbed the first hill, but there no chaise was ; the next, but there no chaise was ; nor yet at the third. So trudging on and on, ascending hill after hill, bent upon taking news back that would ease his fair guest, he had travelled several miles from home, when —ah!—he was aware of an old horse. The old horse was feeding quietly on the roadside between broken traces, and did not deign to raise a head to scan his fellow-passenger.'

Fearing the truth, Geoffrey hastened his steps ; he broke into a run, until at no great distance he reached a turn in the road. There lay the carriage beside the wall, broken and overturned, its wheels idle in the air ; and in the midst of the ruin the driver, his limbs relaxed, his livid face thrown back without a sign of life.   Justly alarmed to see the man so still, Geoffrey ran up, rent his neckcloth away, raised his head, felt for his pulse.

"Alas, he is dead ! Is he dead ? His pulse, it beats faintly ! Ah, no ! Yes ! He breathes ! he lives ! "

Rushing wildly off, and breathlessly searching hither and thither, Geoffrey returned after a few minutes, that seemed too long by hours, with his hat full of precious water. On its first application the man was a little roused, stirred his limbs, and uneasily murmured words that could not be caught.

Then he began to raise his head a little, fancying himself, poor man, still on his cushion, for he shakes his left hand, as if it still handled the reins, and muttering, " Gee up, y' old jade, gee up," lashes out on his right with a will, but no whip.

" He is delirious," thought Geoffrey. However, another dose of water caused him to sit up, lolling between his straddling legs, and staring bewildered around. There-

upon our friend, much easier in mind, proceeded to feel his limbs in scientific fashion in
order to ascertain what bones were fractured,
joints dislocated, or other injuries sustained.
His right leg was discovered to be sound ; so
far so well. The left was under examination,
when the unfortunate coachman, who had been
momentarily becoming more alive, and now
began to take particular notice of his
benefactor, suddenly with a defiant oath
threw out his left fist, catching him such a
blow on the nose as sent him sprawling yards
along the road. He got up again with his
bloody face and dusty back, fully convinced
that his patient was out of danger; so taking
the remainder of the water, he soused him
with a vengeance, and fetched him staggering
to his feet.

After giving the man (no other than
drunken Bob Midgett, once well-known in all
that country, now perchance forgotten)
a fair time to collect himself and shake
his dripping hair, his guardian persuaded
him, partly by convincing reason, partly
by force, to mount the old nag, which
he became like a sack of oats. So they all

three set off towards Meminy Lodge, each beguiling the way with inward communion, for not one of them spoke a word. The old groom, perhaps, was musing of deep pints and sharp points ; the fourlegged one of oats and Elysium, and a long way thither ; the younger man perhaps of—But what is the good ? for who can divine a man's thoughts, unless he be at least a middling medium or spiritual go-between ? what men call pandars in some similar matters.

The whole household turned out to welcome the procession, wondering to see the cha-rioteer reclining helpless on his steed, led by their own chief with a warlike bloody coun-tenance. But their fears were soon allayed ; Bob Midgett and the beast were handed over to Jacob ; and then Geoffrey turned to Miss Hartwell, who had heard, with much annoy-ance, that she was to pass another night in a bachelor's establishment. As his sister was to return in the afternoon of the next day, he would have had her give up all intention of departing. To this Hannah joined her voice, but the young lady was persistent.

" Well," he said at last, " there will, at

least, be no difficulty, for you will be able to return in the carriage that brings my sister up."

Nothing was less in her mind; and she expressed so anxious a desire to leave as early as possible, that it was necessary to promise that Bob Midgett should be sent off on his nag at daybreak to bring up for her whatever conveyance he could obtain. Then they separated.

CHAPTER IX.

THE next morning broke. I might say how in many pages, did not most of my readers already know. Mr. Cantrell, instead of amusing himself by walking or fishing, or in some other country way, as was his wont, remained idly within doors. But before an hour had passed he happened to meet Miss Hartwell, as she glided quickly across the hall. He did not avoid her; she could not avoid him; therefore she was obliged, ill-pleased, I fear, to stand and receive his greeting and to return it. Then as she was quickly going, better pleased I fear, "Stay," he cried, pointing through the open door at something on the distant road, "may not that be your chaise?"

She stopped to look; but for what could be distinguished it might have been the great Lord Mayor's coach, Tim the carrier's donkey, or Agamemnon's own turn-out.

"You would see better from the bottom of the lawn," suggested Mr. Cantrell; though

a person of his judgment should have con-
sidered that Bob Midgett could not possibly
have returned by that hour. Miss Hartwell,
being less informed, could not refuse to be
eager; but as they approached, no, it was
not the Tattleby chaise, it was a muck-cart
going the opposite way. Mr. Cantrell, no
whit crestfallen, declared in several long
sentences, woefully interspersed with other
matter not worth recording, that he had
strictly enjoined on Bob the utmost diligence,
he had stringently commanded Bob and so
forth, he had strictly ordered Bob, etcetera,
and that therefore he would doubtless appear
sometime. Miss Hartwell briefly thanked him
for his voluminous care, and would leave him.

But stay again. Did not Miss Hartwell
see something yonder on the road? Nothing
whatever; Mr. Cantrell must have very good
sight. Yes, after watching a minute, there
might be something; certainly something.
It drew nearer and nearer still under their
eyes. It was not the Tattleby chaise; it was
Jacob returning from the fields.

The morning was very lovely, as fresh as
if it had been the first of all. Miss Hart-

well assented to this, and to several other
things ; but it was time that she returned to
the house. Again her attention was be-
spoken. Certainly something. Shortly there
was seen, not the Tattleby chaise, but two
horsemen, who nevertheless turned up the
house-lane. While Geoffrey was concluding
that they were travellers astray or in search
of information, they had reached the garden
gate, where they in turn caught sight of the
lady and her companion, and saluted them
with as much cordiality as could be manifested
at eighty yards' distance. Then they dis-
mounted and proceeded to tie their horses to
the gate-post.

"Who are these gentlemen, Miss Hartwell ?
They seem to be acquainted with one of us;
which is not myself, I believe."

She began, "They are two gentlemen"—
when, in spite of all her resistance, she was
interrupted by an outburst of tears and
laughter.

Geoffrey knew not whether to understand
something sorrowful or merry. He said
what he ought to compose her, but before he
could conduct her to a seat, which seemed

necessary, the two strangers came up and greeted her both respectfully and heartily. Repressing herself as much as she was able, she managed to listen to their compliments, and give them each her hand. But no sooner did she again loosen her mouth to address her host—" These gentlemen, Mr. Cantrell "— than the paroxysm returned with increased violence, so shaking her slight frame that Geoffrey was obliged to use the assistance of one of the gentlemen to lead her back to the house.

She was delivered up to the housekeeper's attentions, and after the application of restoratives, was seen to be regaining equanimity. Then Geoffrey took the wondering newcomers into another room, and began to question them. One was a thickset, bushy-whiskered man, in dark rough-spun clothes; the other tall and thin, having a tuft of hair under his chin like a goat, and a nose as prominent in his conversation as in his countenance.

When they were seated, Mr. Cantrell said, " You seem to be friends of Miss Hartwell's, gentlemen."

"Of no long standing," answered the taller of them, "though we should be sorry not to be reckoned among her friends."

"That being so," said Geoffrey, "since it is a matter of some consequence, may I ask how far your acquaintance does go?"

"Certainly," the same gentleman replied. "This gentleman is Captain Smiles, of the *Puffer* steam packet, in which I had the honour of crossing the Atlantic in Miss Hartwell's company. I am an American, sir, and my name is Hatcher. As I followed my profession of physician among the steerage passengers, I met with Miss Hartwell engaged in beautiful unprofessional ministrations. I assure you that small pains would have persuaded those poor people of an angel's advent to their relief. From our so working together some intimacy sprang up, and she was kind enough to assure the Captain, who had seconded her charities with ready zeal—"

"Easy, Doctor, easy;" growled Captain Smiles uneasily, "talk about yourself."

"I say she assured the Captain and myself that in case of our presenting ourselves to

Mr. Hartwell, her grandfather, we should meet with a welcome. I hope that gentleman is in good health."

" You will be sorry," said Mr. Cantrell, " to hear that he is no more."

" Is it indeed so?" said the American. " I fear it is a sad blow to Miss Hartwell; she was evidently much attached to him."

Then their host, inviting their attention, gave them the whole of Miss Hartwell's story, so far as he knew it. The strangers listened carefully, and when he had finished, gave an uneasy look the one at the other, and then dropped their eyes. Again they looked, and Captain Smiles opened his mouth to speak, but said nothing. At length Dr. Hatcher began cautiously measuring his words with an inch rule—

" It is a strange story, sir, that you tell us, and I cannot sufficiently pity the young lady. In unprincipled hands she would have been at a dreadful disadvantage, but with the honourable gentleman that you appear to be, I cannot doubt that her honour was safe."

"Sir," replied Geoffrey very gravely, " her honour was never in danger."

The American bowed, and then said, "Well, sir, whatever slight claim we might have had upon Mr. Hartwell's consideration, we have no excuse to be any burden to you; yet I hope, since you say Miss Hartwell purposes staging to-day to some city in this locality, that you will allow us to remain and escort her thither."

"Certainly," replied Mr. Cantrell; "but having done that I shall try to prevail on you to make a longer stay. As far as my poor house permits, I will undertake to fulfil Miss Hartwell's promise, that you would find a welcome here."

When both gentlemen had acknowledged the courtesy without certainly accepting it, they went with their host to enquire after the lady. They were admitted to her presence, and found her recovered, though still showing traces of emotion.

After receiving their sympathy, she said, "Mr. Cantrell will have related to you my present circumstances?"

"Entirely," they replied.

"You know then," she said, "how impossible it is for me to make even the small return I wished for your many kindnesses to me."

"I don't know, Miss Mercy," quoth the Captain, "what kindness you are talking about. I know it was an honour to have you to set foot on my vessel; and" (this in a louder voice), "she's carried herself a mighty deal prouder since, I can tell you."

Seeing her smile a little, the Yankee added, "It is so, I assure you. To my knowledge she has since given a wider berth to several former intimates, and regularly cut a vulgar little tug boat that tried to make up to her."

While they were laughing, Geoffrey put in, "Miss Hartwell, cannot you prevail on these gentlemen to let me take up and endorse your invitation, which seems otherwise likely to be dishonoured? Your friends shall be as free to this house as if it were your own."

"I am afraid," answered Mercy, yet greatly pleased, "that I am already under too deep obligations to you; but if the Captain and Dr. Hatcher would like to remain a day or two in our country, they need not fear an entertainment for their own sakes."

On Geoffrey turning to them, the Doctor

then said, "When an offer has been made so kindly, and supported so gracefully, it would be a brutality not to accept it, if possible. What do you say, Captain ? "

" The same," said Captain Smiles.

So they agreed ; and then leaving Miss Hartwell, went out while luncheon was preparing, to find what amusement they could in viewing the situation of the house.

CHAPTER X.

MEANWHILE Roger Bonifant had passed through
Tattleby, calling, for some reason or other, at
the station, and thence tramped the dusty road
to Meminy Lodge. He entered unnoticed;
for at that time Cantrell and his new guests
were occupied in another direction. Having
looked into the dining and breakfast-rooms,
and found no one in either (he might better
have tried the cellar than the drawing-room),
he dragged himself upstairs to his own
chamber. There dropping his knapsack and
hat in slovenly, weary fashion on to the floor,
he sat down on the edge of the bed for a
good while, thoughtfully whistling and swing-
ing his heels. At length he rose, and thoughtfully began to wash off his dusty weariness.
That done, he proceeded, still thoughtfully,
to empty the knapsack. He drew forth a
pair of socks, a night-gown, a small brush
and comb, and one or two other articles
grateful to the body of man, and placed them
on the bed beside him; and finally a little

Bible; and he turned to the fly-leaf, on which was inscribed in flimsy, girlish scrawl, the name of Constant Cantrell, dated many years back. Dated back to when they were children, and he and she and Geoffrey played together all day in the sunshine, and thought of nothing, not even of their play, but still played on, and thought not.

Many men have tears in their eyes as they think of their childhood; perhaps more than for any dead friend. And no wonder if the spirit of their childhood has died as well as the body, for two deaths are there. We cannot see whether it is so with Roger, for he has put up the book into his pocket, and has gone to look through the window.

How comforting is the sight of the cheerful sunlight on the grass; the white-flecked sky in which one lark is singing; the breeze—that frolicsome, outlandish child, born far beyond the sea—and all the doings of Nature, often written down, never described! How many would die heart-broken did they not have consolation, whence they know not, whither they look not, or, looking, look unwittingly. Sympathy enwraps us like the air; support lies under us wide and firm as the earth. We are ever in leading-strings. Our father is ever by us; our mother is always nursing us, always humouring us and hushing us. We rest upon her lap when we think we lie forsaken; she holds our hand, though we think we walk alone. We are never left, not one of us; not for a moment left.

But Roger quits the window and the room, and as he is going, says to himself, "A strange woman! I would have sworn that she cared no more for my body or my soul than to consign one to the grave and the other to the devil and be rid of them; and yet—Mercy on us, who is this?"

Mercy, indeed, whom he crossed at the stair-head as she came down by another passage. She returned his bow, but was at the bottom of the stairs before he was ready with any further advance. Roger went down in a muse. There was no one in the hall to question, and, being too weary or too lazy to seek, he sat down on the first chair to think it out.

Assuredly this was no companion of Miss Cantrell's, for he knew that she had not yet arrived. Who then was she? "Well," he concluded at last, "whatever it be, good or ill, Geoffrey will have the credit, which I do not grudge him; and I the blame, which nobody will grudge me; and Constant will love us both more dearly than before." Surely the grindstone had been used terribly before Roger Bonifant's tongue took so sharp an edge.

However, his mind had scarcely been made up, before it was taken to pieces again by the entrance of Geoffrey and his guests. After greetings passed the latter immediately went upstairs to prepare for lunch, and Geoffrey profited by their absence to give Roger a short account of the last four days' events very soberly, and with little attention to quizzing questions.

When he had concluded, "Still," said Roger, " after all your elaborate explanations it is by no means clear to me that you might not have got rid of this young lady much sooner. What, a shower of rain, a drunken coachman, a bit of headache keep her here four or five days?"

"What could I do?" replied Geoffrey,

somewhat indignantly. "Would you have had me turn a sick girl out into a tempest of rain and thunder, and bid her trudge sixteen miles up hill and down hill to Tattleby?"

"Certainly not, if not agreeable to yourself."

"Then it was not agreeable to me," said Geoffrey emphatically.

"My dear fellow," answered Roger, laughing, "I saw that from the beginning."

"And might have understood it without seeing."

"After seeing the lady. A very pretty girl, Geoffrey."

"You are of my opinion."

"You might have said, 'I am of your opinion,' but of course you appropriate to yourself all opinions relating to her. A very pretty girl."

"I have said so, and am still of the same opinion."

"Not uninteresting to the manly heart that is void of care and every other amusement."

"So it may prove. I will tell you something, Roger."

"You have been trying this five minutes,

R

but have not told me half as much as I have guessed."

"You will guess wrong; you had better give it up."

"Well, what is it?"

"I confess that I am interested in the girl, Roger."

"Thank you for telling me; I should never have found it out of myself."

"Honestly interested."

"Honesty is the best policy—for a life-insurance—that is to say, for matrimony."

"Without taking the character of a prying busybody, which I hate."

"Hey? I thought you were to speak of love."

"I leave that to others, whom there are."

"What, there are several of you? How many are accepted, how many in despair?"

"Pray, listen reasonably."

"Meaning ever, listen and not reason."

"Just so," said Geoffrey, turning at length; "for you never reason rationally. You call it reasoning, when you are madder than usual. What do you know of reason? Did you see it perhaps in your infancy?"

" I had no chance, for I kept company
with you."

" How blind then you were to your
chances ! "

" It's true that I never saw them."

" How should you discern them ; you, who
call a hare's capers the discourse of reason ?"

" Or you, who call an elephant's stern the
seat of reason ? "

" Reason's a sterner thing than you think,
Roger Harebrain."

" Then I'll gladly be quit of it."

" Do so, and listen to me."

" That would be a pretty quitting of
reason."

" Ay, a quittance, as you say, and after due
receipt too. Now have done."

" You are done up."

" Not a whit ; I could give you quittance
all day on so reasonable a topic, jest for jest."

" Yes, you do sometimes talk reasonably
in jest. Your jokes savour of reason, as if
they had been dipped in it after the making."

" If yours are dipped they are drowned ;
they come out dead, not dyed. But now—"

" You are always their chief mourner."

"Because I alone survive them; I have become habituated. But now, but now," he continued hurriedly, as Roger opened his mouth for another discharge, "listen, Roger, listen. If I give your thoughts a moment's start I shall never overtake them, so light they are. And for you to misunderstand me in this might turn out a serious matter."

"Upon my word, my dear fellow," Roger answered, "you are more serious in it than I thought."

"Please not to mistake this," said Geoffrey with great firmness, "that my chief reason in urging Dr. Hatcher and Captain Smiles to stay, was the hope that it would lead to Miss Hartwell's being provided for."

"I understand perfectly; one will give her away, the other will be your best man. If I may advise, the Captain has the more fatherly appearance."

"Pray drop your absurdity for a while and be unnatural," said Geoffrey, getting a little heated. "Perversity is not wit, or only its tangled ends and ragged waste. You are well aware that I speak of the gentlemen's own inclinations towards the lady; of which

I am fully convinced, having observed their behaviour."

Roger cast his eyes up, and murmured as if to himself—

"All the world knows the fate of two Kilkenny cats; but when there are three?" Then turning to his friend he enquired in dulcet tones, "And you have also observed the lady's own inclinations?"

"No, I have not," Geoffrey answered shortly.

"You have not?" Roger solemnly repeated, wagging his head.

"Do you suppose that for these three or four days I have always been hanging on to her?"

"You might hang on to a worse peg, Geoffrey. And by the way, I think you said her name was Margaret."

"I did not," said Geoffrey. "I have not mentioned her name."

"Well, what is it? Of course you know."

"It is Mercy."

"A very merciful name; and she will have mercy."

Perhaps it was well for peace that the

strangers returned before Geoffrey could reply. The gentlemen proceeded at once to the dining-room. But their repast ended, they were glad again to seek the cool of the hall, where they arranged themselves at will on the seats and stairs in various lazy attitudes. Geoffrey, seeing his guests sufficiently amused by his cigars and Mr. Bonifant's gaiety, sat a little apart, and appeared sometimes to be listening effortless to their conversation, and now to be wholly in thought. Perhaps he was balancing the rival claims of the American doctor and English captain to Miss Hartwell's hand. As an Englishman, of course he could not but prefer an Englishman to win her; but for her own part her only desire was for the chaise, which still came not.

CHAPTER XI.

It is now three minutes past four by the sun, which keeps Greenwich time, and ten minutes to five by the old hall clock, which keeps its own time, when Constant Cantrell drives up to the house, and no sounds are heard save those that are usually heard at that hour and season in the country. She comes in unobserved except by old Jacob, who hobbles up to hold the horse, and exchange a touch of the hat for a smile. The following accounts for this seeming neglect and also for Bob's failure to return. When Constant reached Tattleby she found that one of the "Peacock's" horses was already engaged, and the other, it was doubted, was in some way injured in nerve or constitution by the late accident; or anyhow, was to be regarded as a dangerous beast for a lady to sit behind with a driver fond of his cups. Therefore, the landlady made shift to borrow the fast young mare of a fast young farmer in the neighbourhood, often seen at the "Peacock," which trotted the lady home an hour before she was expected.

Mercy was patiently fretting the hours away close to the society of her aged friend, when she heard the arrival, and ran to the side-door to look. Miss Cantrell was just entering. At her astonished gaze, when self-restraint was for the moment surprised, the timid girl shrank back, blushing and abashed, though scarcely knowing why. The other lady passed on into the house.

Roger's merriment, gradually rising, had dissipated the sadder thoughts of his new-found companions, until he had drawn them on to add the chorus to a song, which he trolled lustily forth—

The mind is a man's within,
  Whatever the weather without,
Though the wind at the casement din,
  And the rain run over the spout.
Then button your coat up to your chin,
  And cheerily look outside;
For if the heart is warm within,
  Frost cannot bite the hide.

The mind is a man's within,
  Whatever the weather without;
Though the wind at the casement din,
  And the rain run over the spout.
So let us whistle under breath,
  When we may not whistle aloud,
And care not for our garment's scaith,
  Elbowing through the crowd.

They had raised their voices in a final chorus, more lusty than musical—

> For the mind is a man's within,
> Whatever the weather—

when Miss Cantrell appeared before them. The two strangers cut their note off with a yapping wail, like a dog's checked howl, and rose to their feet; while Roger, affecting to see nothing, finished the verse solo—

> without ;
> Though the wind at the casement din,
> And the rain ran over the spout.

Then he also arose, exclaiming—

" Miss Cantrell ? Wonderful ! "

Geoffrey had given his sister an affectionate welcome, which was, perhaps, less lovingly returned than usual, and was now introducing to her the strangers, who were received with almost as icy a politeness as Mr. Bonifant himself was accustomed to.

"Old friends of yours, Geoffrey, I suppose?" she said.

" New ones," he replied emphatically, " whom I am happy to have gained."

Without a word more, she made her excuses to the gentlemen, and left. She had not seen Roger; at least, she did not notice him, which he took very carelessly. Geoffrey followed her, and was soon engaged for the third time that day in explaining the situation.

The sister listened at first cool and unmoved; but touched in the end by his well-drawn picture of the orphan-girl, seemed disposed to take up what had been done. Delighted to see this, he said—

"I rejoice, my dear Constant, that you approve of the course I have taken. Besides, I have another reason. But I fear you are too indifferent about poor Roger to hear anything."

Her countenance changed, and she said with constraint—

"What have you to say, Geoffrey, about Mr. Bonifant? I suppose you can tell me in a few words?"

"In a very few," he replied; and then said rather consciously—

"I hope you will not think me officious or oldwomanish; and, indeed, it's the last character I should care to assume—"

"Mr. Bonifant's, surely," said she. "But you are not complimenting old women."

He would not answer; but, after choosing his word, said again—

"It would be a good thing, Constant, if Roger were to marry."

"For himself or his wife?" she enquired too scornfully.

"Both," he answered; "for if Roger finds a good wife, I do not doubt that she will find a good husband."

"You seem to be disputing the existence of good wives, brother."

"Nay," he answered, looking lovingly down on her, "or what becomes of our good sisters? Shall you always keep your antipathy to him, Constant? I thought that such a marriage as I foresee would remove the greater part of your objections."

"What makes you say that, Geoffrey?" she said; and as she spoke her paleness seemed to whiten.

"Because you are a little inclined to suspicion, Constant, if I may be frank to your only weakness; and his happy marriage I should think would remove the ground of that."

"I do not deny," she said, assenting contradictorily, "that if Mr. Bonifant does marry happily he will be a very different person from what I now consider him. Have you anything more to say? I am a little tired."

"Indeed, my dear, you look really ill. I will not trouble you now. Though the subject is of interest and importance to me, I fear it is of none to you. Another, or any time will do."

"No, no," she answered impatiently, "finish now, and never let me be troubled with it again."

"In my mind, Constant, Roger and Miss Hartwell, if there are no obstacles—as I am aware there may be—would make a very good match; an admirable, a capital match."

Miss Cantrell answered, with more anger than she had shown before—

"I know something of Mr. Bonifant—nothing of this Miss Hartwell; therefore I cannot accuse her in any way of matching him. But you, Geoffrey, are thoroughly acquainted with both."

"At least what I know of her promises

better and better of a better knowledge. I
have it from Roger's own lips that he admires
her."

"Mr. Bonifant?" she answered, in sur-
passing scorn. "Oh, no doubt! He has a
ready prepossession for every woman of
doubtful antecedents."

"And what doubt have you, Constant, of
Miss Hartwell's antecedents?"

"At least," she replied, "I give her the
benefit of a doubt."

"Such a doubt," he answered firmly, "is
no benefit, but an injury and a shame. I
cannot endure even from you—much less
from you—from you it is intolerable, that so
much innocence should be abused. You
would do well to be duly cautious; but you
wear suspicion always like a habit, not an
armour."

"Why do you reproach me?" she said
more faintly. "I am not likely to oppose the
union; I take your word that it is very suit-
able. But I will not take raptures up as if
it were something transcendent; and if you
please, I wish to hear no more of it."

"I thought," he said, deeply angered, "to

find some sympathy with you. In spite of all, I little guessed your spite was such as to contemn his happiness, and even regret his welfare. But I will answer your wish, and say no more about it."

So saying, he left her, though he must have perceived, had he been less angry, that his sister looked very ill, whether from the fatigue of her journey, or the heat of the weather, or whatever other cause.

CHAPTER XII.

When Miss Cantrell came again out of her room, paler, statelier, more contained than ever, she found Mr. Bonifant sitting by himself at the top of the stairs. Why he was there, wherefore should we attempt to say, like some ancient Anaxagoras guessing at the moon? Suffice it that he was there—like the moon—and likely enough something moony. He rose to let her pass, saying, with the gay smile that he could always summon—

"Most happy to see you again, Miss Cantrell."

After a short stay, as if to draw herself up, she replied, in a set, deliberate tone—

"1 am sorry I cannot return the compliment, Mr. Bonifant."

He answered, with a little laugh—

"Pray do not; keep it:" adding, with an earnestness that mocked itself, "and if you can, believe it."

"That I cannot," she replied, nerved for surgery. "You know very well, sir, that I have never desired your residence here, though with no great delicacy you have continued it."

At this beginning, the young man's countenance fell, in spite of bold-hearted efforts.

"You know that I have never admired your conduct; a matter of little moment had you not insisted on intruding your presence. I am compelled to speak plainly. Finally, your introduction of this young woman here is an insult to this house and to myself."

"Was I the author of that?" he cried with wrathful indignation. "If no kindness, at least some scanty justice, if you please."

But Miss Cantrell was regardless; or if she blenched, it was in her heart and nothing in her face.

"I must request you, if you claim to have any honour, to withdraw from this house, with all that belong to you."

Mr. Bonifant, leaning back on the wall and speaking deep, with a strong man's vehement calmness—

"Do you banish me a second time?"

"Since it is necessary," she answered, "I do."

Then he cried, passionately, desperately, even stamping once on the ground—

"Constant, Constant, why will you give a man no chance, while he has any inclination after goodness and you?"

Amazed, she drew back, her paleness pallid. Driven from her calculations, she said not a word.

Roger has spoken his last, and stands looking fire.

At last she raises her head even timidly, and hesitating and trembling says—

"It is not easy to understand you, Mr. Bonifant."

"Is it so difficult?" he flung moodily back. "It is not hard to understand that you hate me; nor hard, I daresay, to find reasons for it."

"I do not hate you, Mr. Bonifant," she said; and her countenance took the tint that roses are tinged with which are called white.

"Your Christian virtues forbid it; I would say, despise."

Again the answer came, low-voiced—

"I cannot despise you, Mr. Bonifant."

"Cannot, though you would? When did

s

you fail before in that ability? Must I say dislike then? A petty word, but not forbidden."

"No," came back, lower still.

"What, are you so scrupulous about words? I wish you would deny the thing too, but that you cannot. We will let it rest here then, weakly enough, that you disapprove of me."

At first there was no answer.

"Yes, that is the word."

Then she replied faintly, "You would misunderstand me if I were to answer."

"Make no answer then. I understand your silence as well, and better."

"No, you do not," she answered in distress.

"What, not even disapproval? Then we can only come to indifference, in which fight more devils than in all the passions there are."

Miss Cantrell could only shake her head helplessly.

"I beg your pardon for the word," he said again, interpreting the action as he would.

Again they stood in silence, until Miss Cantrell spoke with an unsteady, almost daunted voice—

"I see that great mistakes have been made by both of us;" and it was plain even to Roger that she was weeping.

He drew close to her, and stood by her side, and spoke to her. He spoke so low that he was obliged to bend over her, and put his head by hers above her shoulder; so low that even then these words were barely caught, "Why are you troubled, Constant?" That was simply all that could be heard, and if she murmured an answer, it fell softer than the dropping of her tears.

Now this shows my historical honesty, that knowing nothing, I am content to say so little. At any rate, whatever was said or done, was said soon and done quickly; for there were footsteps in the hall below. Constant descended the stairs quietly, composing herself as she went; Roger stayed behind incapable. What strong man can master himself half so dexterously as a feeble woman?—though we have men, brave souls, diplomatically training all their lives to speak and say nothing, to look and show nothing, to smile and mean nothing, not even friendliness, nor even spite.

CHAPTER XIII.

WELL had Mercy Hartwell interpreted Miss
Cantrell's air of astonishment at meeting her,
and on her disappearance had flown into the
yard full of angry shame, hoping to persuade
the driver to return with her at once. Of
course he resisted with a horsey man's stolidity,
averring that he was too much of a Christian
to let his beast go another stage unrested and
unbaited; with a reserved *à fortiori*, doubtless,
with regard to himself. She had therefore to
contain herself with an almost tearful impatience, while solemnly and circumspectly he
ate his meat, and ate his bread and cheese,
and drank his beer to the last. Then throwing himself back on his chair with a full sigh,
he filled his pipe, and smoked it out. That
duty accomplished, he was prevailed on to
hobble out on his ricketty legs and begin to
set the horse to. Hannah was resigned. That
is to say, she repined as folks repine against
fate—tearfully, feebly, hopelessly, with much
groaning, much shaking of the head.

Mercy the while was writing a letter addressed to Geoffrey Cantrell, Esquire; which she directed Hannah to lay in his room, after she was gone. .Then she bade her an affectionate farewell, promising something, evading something ; but as dreading above all an interruption of her departure, entreating her not to follow to the gate. This Hannah would fain have combated, little weening of her mistress's thoughts, but was cut short with an express prohibition, a little cowed to see the usually gentle girl so determined.

Mr. Cantrell was sitting with his guests; but alert with uneasy expectancy he caught a suspicion of what was going on, and came out just in time, as it happened, to see Miss Hartwell set her foot on the gig-step.

" What are you doing, Miss Hartwell?" he called too hastily and vehemently.

She answered quietly yet guiltily—

" Did I not promise to leave you to-day ? " having now gained the cushion.

"But not without a farewell, without a word, surely ? " he said, approaching her.

And she—

" I was wishful not to trouble you. But I was not forgetful; Hannah has something that I have written. If it has an ungrateful appearance, you must pardon me."

" Must you go ? " he asked.

" Yes."

Nothing could be shorter; and like a cord it was the tighter and stricter for it.

"Since it is so, at least let me first say what I wish to say."

Mercy bowed, and set herself to listen.

" Not here," he said; " come with me if only for a minute."

However reluctant, she could not refuse to descend.

He took her back to the house into the empty breakfast-room. There, far from accepting the situation, as the phrase goes, he tried every reason, every contradiction of persuasion to bring her to relent. Never was gentleman so obstinate, so unreasonable with his reasons, for her constant denial was on necessity, rather a complaint than a plea. Neither would she promise as before to go no further than Tattleby, avoiding the question, saying something loosely about the uncertainty of her movements, and only dropping her head the lower, the closer pressed.

At last perplexed, grieved—I dare say with
as many notions in his one head as in a city,
he said, looking narrowly at her—

"It is plain my appeals have no effect. I
wish I knew whether there is any one in the
house who has more influence."

What answer could she make?

"Let me leave you a moment," he said
abruptly; "give me one moment more;" and
left the room, striding hastily towards the
hall.

I cannot say whether he intended to solicit
the aid of the Captain and Doctor, to attempt
a last effort on his sister's sympathy, or to
call in Roger's divinations, or as is most
likely, with no settled purpose whatever,
simply temporising with vexation. But
assuredly he was behaving too passionately
for one who limited his interest.

In the hall he was met by Constant, who
had just descended the stairs. He passed,
without speaking or looking. She spoke; he
neither answered nor turned. He had never
treated her so before. She took him by the
arm, and said in fear—

"What is the matter, Geoffrey?"

"Nothing," he answered, averting his face from her eyes.

"Nothing cannot trouble you so much. Tell me," she pleaded.

"Useless, useless. Nothing need be said, nothing can be done."

"You are angry with me, Geoffrey. Do not be angry with me."

"What cause," he answered, "can I have for that? None surely. Our home is only dishonoured, our name is only disgraced; that is all."

"Tell me what you mean, Geoffrey."

She was in great trouble, but he did not perceive it, for men can see one thing so much as to see nothing ; keen-eyed, even to blindness.

"Do not refuse me, Geoffrey. I have always shared at least your sorrows before."

That was an appeal which he could not disregard. He pointed to the room which he had just left, and said—

"That will tell you all, and more than enough."

She hastened thither. Miss Hartwell was standing in trouble and wonder at Mr. Cantrell's incomprehensible behaviour, doubtful whether not to fly. Constant shut the door. What passed then, in faith, I know well, but it is ladies' secret, revealed only to some several persons upon penalty of divulgement. Therefore let me only say—Not too hasty, pen. But merely this—Consider thy vow. *Sub rosa?* Fie, fie! Under oath of secresy? Like thine own, false heart. Well, for once I will be true, though Grundy die. So, reader, if you please you shall only know this, that in no great while Constant and Mercy came out again, arm-and-arm, heart-and-heart, with gladder faces than either had borne for many a day.

Geoffrey was near the door at the moment that they appeared. Constant led Mercy up to him, and said—

"You may order the gig back to Tattleby, Geoffrey; it will not be wanted to-day."

He made no answer, but his eyes gleamed brief thanks as he went without delay upon the errand.

Hannah was next informed of the change, at which she continued for joy the weeping that she began for sorrow. But shortly, getting a little used to her delight, she began to grudge that it was owing to other persuasions than her own ; so that Mercy was quite ready at her new friend's invitation to go and change her dress. I have been informed, without apparent reason to doubt, that that little toilet took a very considerable time. I only give facts, do not profess to explain them.

When at length the two ladies entered the room in which the gentlemen were, Geoffrey again introduced the Captain and Doctor to his sister, forgetting that he had already done so. She received them graciously, and at once entered into a cordial conversation with them, in which she even allowed Roger to join freely, going so far as to express agreement with him once or twice. Whereat Geoffrey marvelled as much as he had leisure for, being under the necessity of devoting himself to Mercy, who, as he thought, was rather neglected by the others.

Their plain dinner was eaten in mutual concord, and a few minutes after the ladies had withdrawn, Roger proposed to rejoin them. Geoffrey looked knowing, while he assented ;

but his friend stood the brunt with equanimity. The ladies welcomed them.

After a little general conversation Geoffrey, seeing that neither the Captain nor the Yankee attached himself particularly to Miss Hartwell—while Roger seemed rather to pretend a preference for Miss Cantrell's society—felt obliged as host to play the gallant himself.

While those two were talking quietly together, the Doctor said to Miss Cantrell—

"Mr. Bonifant tells us, Miss Cantrell, that you are opposed to the use of wine. I do not deny the evils of its constant employment, but surely a moderate occasional use of it promotes social cheerfulness and enjoyment."

Constant said—

"You mean that it makes one talk more and laugh more, I suppose."

"And generally quickens the life," he added.

"But would a glass of wine assist you in a delicate operation or the consideration of a nice case?"

"I cannot say that it would. But is that the question?"

" I hope it will prove to be the answer. Should you, Captain Smiles, drink wine on seeing your ship in peril in order to escape the better."

"No," said Captain Smiles.

"Or you, Mr. Bonifant, if you wished to—"

Here she stopped short, not knowing how to continue.

" To set the Thames on fire, or light my pipe," said Roger for her with becoming seriousness ; and more solemnly for himself, " Certainly not."

" Then it appears," said she, rescuing the subject from levity, " that even one glass of wine does not make us think or act more clearly, but the contrary. Therefore, if it makes anyone talk more it can only be by making him content to talk more foolishly; if he laughs more it is because he laughs less reasonably ; in short, he is rather less thought-ful than more cheerful. You say that it quickens the life. But how ? By rousing the blood, and stimulating—is it the better emotions or the worse ? "

" Not the very best, I admit," replied the Doctor.

" Does it not make the irritable more irritable, the sensual more sensual, and so, attacking or corrupting the weak place of each, aim in the end at occupying him entirely? And does that promote social intercourse and enjoyment to know that our companions are in a worse mood than ordinary, more brutish or quarrelsome, vainer or weaker, or at least less rational?"

The Doctor made an answer to this, which was doubtless very satisfactory, but unfortunately I am unable to report one word of it.

Soon the American said something which implied that he should take his leave the day following. Constant hoped that he would grant them a longer tenure of his company.

" I fear it is impossible," he said; " I have promised to visit Mrs. Smiles, the Captain's lady, at Lafby, with my wife."

Roger coughed, and turning, looked under sly eyebrows towards Geoffrey, who had also caught what was said, and from him to Mercy. Geoffrey, with a noble fortitude, refused to be abashed, but set it all down in his mind, saying inwardly—

"So much the better for Roger."

After they had drunk tea Constant proposed that they should all walk out together, and while the others were preparing Geoffrey stood alone on the lawn. Suddenly Roger came through the window to him with some great excitement in his eyes, and crying—

"I can throw you now, Geoffrey," took him by the waist and swung him to the ground.

"Are you mad, Roger?" said Geoffrey, rising rather chafed.

Roger with that excitable temperament of his seized his hand and wrung it fiercely, and said in his ear with a whisper that was a compressed shout—

"She loves me, Geoffrey, loves me after all."

"What?" said his friend in amazement, "have you spoken already?"

"I never breathed a word before to-day."

"What?" he cried again, and too loud in his astonishment; "you have met before?"

Roger burst into a wild and gleeful laugh, and laughed loud and long.

"Yes, I have known her some time," he said amid the outburst. "It seems that our two new friends can't interfere. A little blind there, eh, Geoffrey?"

Geoffrey, justly irritated by such vagaries, turned on his heels to go, but was held back by Roger's hand.

"A compromise, Geoffrey! If you prefer Miss Hartwell for yourself—"

No, Geoffrey was determined to go, though he should have to struggle for it.

"Listen, man. I accept in exchange another under this roof in whom we are both interested."

"Constant?" he exclaimed with huge emphasis.

"Yes," answered Constant herself, appearing at the door. "Did you call me?"

"I did," said he, sticking to the truth; in fact, sticking in it, for he got no further.

"What is it?" said she.

"Are you not ready yet?" said he.

"Is that all?" she asked, now alert, glancing her keen, grey eyes from Roger, who did not try to conceal his laughter, to Geoffrey, featuring hurriedly-adjusted composure, like a state personage afforded bare time to robe in. However, nothing more was said, for the

rest of the party came out, and all went forward. Geoffrey walked among them a little
musy, perhaps saying to himself : " I was
convinced, and still am, that some one loves
Mercy Hartwell. If it is not Captain Smiles
nor Dr. Hatcher, nor Roger Bonifant, who
is it ? "

If he really asked himself this question he
probably gave up attempting to answer it,
for he soon turned his attention to his friends,
and Miss Hartwell being nearest at the time,
placed himself beside her. Very little was
said by either of them, but that little was so
engrossing that if I tell you nothing about
the rest of the company, it is likely you will
know as much as they did. In a short time
the country being broken into many knolls and
hollows, the couple, having either advanced
before their companions or dropped behind,
it was uncertain which, were quite out of
sight. Just then, considerately remembering
Miss Hartwell's recent illness, Geoffrey said
to her—

" You had better take my arm; you need
the support."

Miss Hartwell could not with due regard

for her health refuse what was offered in
form so like a prescription. She took it like
a good patient, without a word or grimace.
Then they walked some distance almost in
silence, until they came to a pleasant, grassy
bank which invited Geoffrey to say—

" Let us sit down here and wait for the
others."

Mercy demurred, doubting whether the
others might not be ahead ; but in the end
yielded like a reasonable being to Mr.
Cantrell's arguments.

That waiting really was his object is proved
by his doing nothing else. There he sat looking
fixedly on the grass at his feet, regardless of
his fair companion, who possibly was not interested in grass, but did her best to feign it.

At last, however, he looked up, saying,
as if it were the outcome of his thoughts,
scarcely conscious of a second presence—

" Yes, it is a bad sort of life that I have
led."

If he spoke to himself, still he seemed to
expect Mercy to answer for him, seeing that
he kept his eyes upon her. What could she
say ? She knew nothing, and could deny

T

nothing; therefore she only said simply and timidly—

"But you repent, do you not?"

"While you look at me with those eyes I do."

She had not been thinking of her eyes, or what she was doing with them, but thus reminded, withdrew them hastily.

"Do not take them away; look at me so always."

But she only turned them the more aside.

"Will you not?"

Indeed, Mr. Cantrell was pressing an impossible request very eagerly, to which Mercy, laughing a little and blushing a good deal, replied—

"If two persons stare at one another one of them must be put out of countenance."

Before Geoffrey had thought an answer out the others returned. He took pains to explain, rather at his own prompting than their questions, that he had been awaiting them there, supposing them to be behind.

"Waiting, I see, very patiently," quoth Mr. Bonifant; "for which you have my praise."

Geoffrey could not answer, for he had turned away and was engaged with Dr. Hatcher, remarking on some wild flowers which the latter carried.

They now started homewards; and it happened, at which I cannot wonder enough, that this time Roger and Constant unwittingly dropped behind. I cannot relate all that passed between them, but some time during the separation Roger, taking out of his pocket the little Bible that he had found in the knapsack, said—

"I suppose I ought to return your Bible?"

Constant put up her hand for the book, which he still held out but did not relinquish, answering—

"I think I ought to apologise for allowing them to give you so old a one, but it was the only one in the house small enough."

"Did you not know," said the gentleman, "that I should prefer it a thousand times to the largest family Bible that was never read?"

"If I had thought that likely," answered Miss Constant, "of course I could not have put it—could not have allowed them to put it in."

"And yet it is so true, and has been true so long, that it seems to me like one of the fundamentals that every one must know, which the children learn at school."

I doubt that Miss Cantrell barely listened to him, rather pondering what she said next, delicately, soberly, as dealing with things not of indifferent use—

"I hope you read a little in it sometimes."

"I read very often on the fly-leaf," he answered.

Disapprovingly, but mildly, she said—

"Yet that is the only part not worth reading."

"Including the dedication to the religious King James?"

"Oh, do not jest on so serious a subject, Mr. Bonifant."

"So serious a subject as King James? But he was a merry monarch of serious subjects."

"Not that," she said, "but what we were speaking about, God's Word."

"My dear Constant," and he went closer and spoke deeper, "since it is a serious matter I cannot speak of it at all if not jestingly. It is not in my nature; at least, not in my mood. Let it be; remember the earth's doings, our mother's; her deep things lie deep until inward force upheaves them; nothing outward moves them."

He said no more, but as they went on side by side in the growing twilight began to murmur snatches of song, out of which the following could be barely heard :—

> You are not angry that I love you?
> For I have forced no pains to move you.
>   Yet had it been too hard, if he
> Who loved so much were nothing known;
> But with a little scantly shown,
>   I left you free.
>
> Yet should you anger, even though
> I might ask more than you do owe?
>   Would it not rather be approved,
> That 'twere a cruel destiny,
> For one who loves much not to be
>   A little loved?

CHAPTER XIV.

The next day the Captain and Doctor departed. A happy journey to them, and bright smiles from their wives at its end!

In the evening of the same day as the remaining quartette sat together, Geoffrey announced his intention of going up to London.

"How is that, Geoffrey?" asked Constant, in disquiet.

"I am wearying," he answered, "of an idle life. Besides, if I do not take to the law, I fear it will lie on my conscience that an excellent pleader is lost to the world."

"You are very scrupulous," said Roger, "to consider us so tenderly. Your christianly example moves me to be your companion to London."

"The best thing in the world," answered Geoffrey, "for you. In Lincoln's Inn you shall have my counsel and countenance."

"Am I waste ground for you to shoot your rubbish in? Trespassers will be prosecuted. Thanking goodness for the escape, Paternoster

Row will be my inn, a hostelry that receives many a footsore wayfarer, and dismisses him heartsore."

"Tush, man, it will go no further than corns and bunions with you; your heart is whole enough. Unless some one knows anything to the contrary."

Geoffrey added this, looking curiously round.

"As sound as your own, Geoffrey," said Roger, slapping his chest, and looking round as curiously.

Constant, not ill-pleased, I believe, enquired—

"Do you seriously mean to make an attempt in literature?"

"I take my cue from the publisher," he answered. "If he means it seriously, I mean it merrily; if he takes it for a joke, I am all solemnity."

"If I try to dissuade you, my dear fellow," said Geoffrey, "it is in your own interests, not mine; for I am not obliged to read what you choose to write. Throw in your lot with me. You have no experience, a commodity impoverishing to buy, ruinous to neglect. I shall know my time to a day; your apprentice-term will be long, the premium heavy, and neither fixed. Remember poor Lofty, who could never make a livelihood by writing till he died. Then his widow gained a fortune by his copyrights, and married his publisher."

"I have served half my time already," said Roger. "Do you think I have been quite idle this last year? If I am not known to fame and famine yet, I have some acquaintance with editors and money orders."

"On your sacred word as a genius? Pray in what form do you enlighten us?"

"Pretty nearly all except travels. History, philosophy, science, fiction, poetry have all been adorned."

"A poet too, O Dan Chaucer? Won't you favour us with a glimpse of what is to be the prevailing mode?"

"Do you fancy that I carry my pockets stuffed with reams like a Dominie Sampson?"

Constant took it up with a reproving glance at her brother—

"If you have anything that you can show us, we shall be very glad indeed to see it."

He handed her a small piece of paper, saying—

" This is all that I have with me. I think I could show you something better, but," he added low for her only, " but nothing truer."

She took the sheet and looked through it; but refused Geoffrey's challenge to read it aloud, passing it to Mercy on her left. The latter perused it, exclaimed, "How beautiful!" and then handed to Geoffrey the following—

I.

How happy might one be
   Of winning merits and persuasive tongue
   And aspect manly young,
Being as near as I have been to thee!

How happy would he be;
   For he could boldly apprehend success
   By venturing no less,
When he was near as I have been to thee.

II.

If it were not bold
   To hope that any lady would commit
All of her royal worth into my hold
Without a thought
   Of ever recovering it,
Then I might love indeed ; but not, if not.

If the hazard were
   Not far too wild, that I in due degree
Might be advanced your lord high treasurer
Doubtful of naught
   To break my dignity,
Then might I love indeed ; but not, if not.

In a few days the friends went down to London. They put out the following years to honest work, which repaid them fully with interest. Meanwhile, Constant and Mercy lived together sisterwise in Northumberland. The end of all was the twofold marriage, which I saw at Purley.

THE TUG OF WAR.

THE day's duties were over at Wackington Grammar School. The scholars were all abed, dreaming of mischief; and we were at leisure—the French master and I, who were " on duty " that day—to light our pipe or cigarette and sit down, stretching our legs and tongues before the fire. At first, I believe, we were chatting of Virgil, about whom our good Frenchman had many opinions to offer; for had he not read a translation ? But somehow we soon came round to the late war between France and Germany. Everything fell *à propos* of that to M. Droit. Boots reminded him of French contractors, blacking of German detractors. I was not fond myself of the subject, whose freshness had long been smudged with much handling, and I eased my feelings in a warlike denunciation of war. Monsieur listened to me patiently for several minutes—in fact, until his cigarette was puffed out—and then, tapping my arm with two fingers, said—

"Stay a minute, my friend."

Being well-nigh breathless, I acknowledged the reasonableness of the request, and ceased to brandish my hand and my eloquence, returning that to my pocket, this to my pipe.

"You say," quoth he, "that war makes great evils. Quite true; anger, robbery, murder, brutality, waste of wealth, energy, men, and so forth. Quite true. But is it that war brings forth only evil? Does it not also evoke our most secret virtues, as the blacksmith's hammer drives heat out of the cold iron; summoning courage heroic in the gentlest woman, abundant tenderness in the roughest men?"

"What," I just murmured, "of our secret unproductive vices that it also calls into devilish activity?"

But he would not hear me, as he dashed miles ahead to the same old tune; which to rehearse would make this little canzonet as long and heavy as an oratorio. Sophistical arguments, moreover, to which a schoolboy might play Socrates. But no! I was too lazy then, having once settled down, to take my friend in the flank, and will be too chivalrous now to attack him in the rear. Having said much, he related a tale in support thereof, for the truth of which he vouched his own word. Sorry I am that I cannot reproduce his picturesque phraseology and lively gesticulation, his ardent description of the maiden's charms, his impatient indignation against the German, his fiery admiration of the French, his frowns, his smiles, his sneers, the curl of his lip, the twirl of his moustache, above all his laugh, blithe, scornful or grim. Alas, all are gone. The soul is away; the body only remains, which I proceed to bury decently in my British jog-trot style.

It was the beginning of the Franco-German war. The Germans, feebly threatened with invasion, had drawn first blood, and driven the ill-prepared forces of their enemy over the Vosges Mountains to the Sarre. There they rallied under Marshal MacMahon, and fought the famous battle of Worth. The day, which began happily, almost victoriously, for the French, closed, as the German troops grew to overwhelming numbers, in repulse and rout. Among the last to cease resistance was a little company posted on a spur of the steep range that rises from the left bank of the river. Originally five hundred, reduced to fifty, they were summoned to surrender by a captain of Uhlans. They received the summons with cries and gestures which seemed to be mistaken by the German for acceptation. Anyhow he rode up gently at the head of his troop, but was shot dead by a young Frenchman, who stood in advance of his comrades. Furiously the Uhlans galloped up the slope, a thousand men. Our captain-slayer was hurled at the first shock down a ravine that skirted the hill; the rest were cut to pieces. Night fell, covering death and life, dismay and exultation with the same shroud.

In a quiet place, five or six miles from the battlefield is Heimstadt, a great low-backed mansion, where a wealthy land-owner dwelt, named Meyer; a worthy old man, tall and strong beyond any of his neighbours, full of honest health and simple dignity. His wife was dead, and his only daughter, Margaret, was a girl of sixteen, fair as the day, lustrous as the sun, clad in golden hair that hung down her back, and adorned much more with a thousand lasting graces. Moreover, she could manage a dairy, cook a *ragoût*, and make coffee with most. Such were the charms of Margaret Meyer; a fair face, a rich dowry, a good conscience, and the best receipt for a *potage* in all Lorraine.

As the battle was waged, the voice of the artillery could be heard like a dull blaspheming mutter as far as Heimstadt, and was harkened to with dreadful interest, as a gamester strains his bloodshot eyes to watch the course of his last desperate stake. The household tried to go about their daily work, but were apt to knot themselves into frightened clusters and stand listening. How goes the fight? In vain the stout-hearted master urged them to their duties, and laughingly scouted the notion of defeat. His presence was a momentary hope, that fell into deeper dread on his withdrawal. Everything was out of joint; the labourer did not go afield, the milk lay unskimmed in the dairy, even dinner was forgotten. Where was Margaret? Clinging constantly to her father, and catching a courage from his brave eye that she trembled to lose in his absence.   So the day passed in sickly doubt.   The cannon gradually ceased; night fell, and quiet came, but not rest.

How had the fight gone?   Remote from the highways, they saw no one to inform them; could only sit together questioning their own ignorance until they were pale with speculation.   No one durst go to bed.

Far in the night a knock was heard at the door.   None would open at command, threat or entreaty, so that at last M. Meyer was obliged to go himself.   Boldly he flung the door open, and then, shading his candle with one hand from the wind, dimly saw something before him—a man, a soldier, uniform French, weaponless.

"Who is it?" he called.

" A French soldier, sir."

" How come you here?" asked M. Meyer, thinking that this must be a deserter.

" Don't you know that the day has gone against us ?"

" What do you mean ?"

" The Prussians were five to one. We have lost; that is all."

M. Meyer will not believe it. This is some deserter, with a colourable tale. He will detain him till he has communicated with the authorities.

"Enter, soldier," said he.

The soldier limps after him to the great kitchen, where all the house is gathered. There he is eagerly scanned. A slim, stooping figure, with pale, beardless face, grimy and desperate; uniform clay-soiled and tattered, round his arm a bloody handkerchief.

It was impossible to reject a testimony sworn so eloquently, and M. Meyer struck his brow with horror.

"We have lost!"

All heard the hoarse whisper. The women shrieked; the men turned pale. But a blessed relief came in charity, for the young soldier sank fainting to the ground.

"Run, Marie, for water. Jean, fetch brandy. Linen, Margaret."

Under their treatment the patient soon revived. The wound on the arm was found to be a pretty severe sword-cut, but not dangerous. The faintness sprang as much

W

from fatigue and hunger as from loss of blood.

Food was set before him. At first he was too hungry to eat; but after a few sips of the brandy, and a few minutes' repose of those weary limbs, he managed to swallow a mouthful. That opened the way for more, and he finished by making a prodigious meal. It was easy to believe, as he said, that he had not tasted food that day.

When he had eaten what he could, M. Meyer began to question him about the battle.

He could tell but little, having been too intent on his own rifle to watch the rest. They had fought as long as they could, and then—

He was choked, struggled to proceed, finally laid his unwounded arm on the table and his head on his arm and sobbed outright. All wept with him, and Margaret most of all.

When they were calm again, and the soldier looked up, M. Meyer questioned him as to his own escape.

He told them shortly that in the last charge a Uhlan officer had cut him on the arm, and the shock of a following steed had flung him down a ravine, beside which he stood. Fortunately, however, his fall was broken by the bushes that clung to the sides of the hollow, and he reached the bottom with little more injury than a bruised hip. After lying stunned for a few minutes, he was able to get on his knees and look about, and then crawl into cover. There he bandaged his wounds; and, night coming on, rose to his feet and stumbled along, heavy in head and sick at stomach, until he had passed the enemy's pickets, yet irregularly placed. He crawled a few more miles—he scarcely knew how— and then found himself there, where he must ask relief, or die.

Having ended his tale amid universal lamentation, he was taken by his host to the best bed in the house. A moment, for very pleasure, he lay awake between the sheets, thinking of Paradise, and then fell asleep.

No sleep for the rest of the house. Under Margaret's oversight some were cleaning and mending the soldier's uniform; others preparing breakfast and a bundle of necessaries against his departure, which must be early for fear of the Prussians. So were the active engaged; the unnerved were busier still with their fears.

But this prosperous bustle was ere long broken by the tramp of approaching horse-men and the sound of military commands. The troopers halted, and the bolted door was summoned by a heavy boot and a loud foreign voice. M. Meyer bade his daughter with-draw to her chamber, and then again went to the door. He beheld a dark group of some twenty cavalry-men, heavily cloaked, whose steaming horses and spiked helmets shone faintly in the moonlight. Germans!

Their leader, in an authoritative voice, cried—

" Show my men to the stables, and then let refreshments be served for them."

For all his proud thoughts, angry eye, and scornful lip, M. Meyer, for other sakes than his own, must needs comply. Calling a ser-vant, he bade him lead the way to the stables, while he himself returned to the kitchen, fol-lowed by the officer. The frightened domestics were huddled of a heap, like sheep in a storm. The master roused them as well as he could, and gave orders that the best in the house should be spread out. It is ill starving armed hunger.

The German, satisfied with the arrangements, was leaving, to take a quieter repast by himself in a parlour, when unhappily he clapped eye on the uniform drying before the fire.

"What is this?" he asked sharply, scanning each face that turned to him.

Before anyone had replied, tramp, tramp, clank, clank, in file the troopers, filling the place with their martial swagger.

"How came this here?" again he asked sternly of Mathurine, the cook, who cowered nearest.

What she would have replied, if anything, was interrupted by M. Meyer, ready now with a story.

"This coat, sir, belongs—"

"Silence, sir," said the officer.

"Belongs to a son—"

"Silence," shouted the officer.

"Hear me, sir, this—"

"Remove him," cried the German; and the old gentleman was forthwith led out.

Mathurine was again more fiercely questioned, and had said enough when, betwixt
sobbing, trembling and bowing, she breathed
the word, " soldier."

" A Frenchman ? Show the way. Waack,
take three men and secure him."

Crippled with terror, the poor woman
tottered out, followed by the soldiers' impatient strides.

*   *   *   *   *

Margaret, when she left the kitchen, had
gone straight to their guest's room and
knocked ; knocked again and listened ; again
more boldly, with hand and foot, calling as
loud as she dare. Still he did not awake.
There was no time to hesitate. She entered,
went up to the bed, and shook him roughly
from his sleep.

" The Prussians are here ! "

He leapt up. " My clothes, where are my
clothes ? "

" I will fetch them," she replied, and flew
downstairs. But as she reached the kitchen
door, she heard a strange voice loud within,
paused suddenly on the threshold, and look-

ing stealthily through espied the German officer. Back she darted upstairs, too much occupied to fear; snatched out a suit of her father's, the first to hand, and ran with them to the young man.

"Quick," she said, "put on these; the Prussians are already in the house. Tell me when you are ready. I wait outside."

The clothes provided would not have been a tight fit for double his girth; however, he blundered into them as he could in the dark, and was soon at the door. The tramp of heavy boots resounded through the house.

"Follow me," whispered a sweet voice; and a dim shape glided ahead.

"Who is it?" he asked, as he followed.

"That matters not; tread more softly."

"Can it be that mademoiselle has deigned—"

"Hush, hush," she replied; "you are not safe yet. Down these stairs, quietly."

They were half-way down, and Margaret's heart was beating at the nearness of escape, when suddenly they heard hasty feet in the passage below. They stopped doubtfully, retreated a step or two; then all at once a lantern shone full upon them, revealing also four soldiers at the foot of the staircase, revolvers in hand.

"Stand!" cried the sergeant.

Seeing no better, they suffered themselves to be seized. Whereupon the captain, surprised to hear the challenge so near, also came forth and at once marked the young lady.

"Who is this?" he said.

"Taken, sir," replied the sergeant, "while assisting the male prisoner to escape."

"Who are you?" he asked of the girl herself.

"Margaret Meyer, the daughter of your host."

"You look dangerous, mademoiselle, but I let you go on condition that you grant a truce to us young men's hearts."

He then told off two men to conduct the young Frenchman to a small room adjoining his own.

"What are you going to do with him?" asked Margaret, eagerly.

"We shall put him in a place where his head will be kept safe from cannon-balls for a month or two, until the war is over. Oh yes, we will take great care of him for you, mademoiselle. He has lost flesh lately I see; but he shall be fattened up again to fit his clothes."

" You will not—not shoot him then ? " she said faltering.

" Bah, we don't shoot prisoners of war; we have better use for powder."

The Frenchman begged to be allowed to resume his uniform. The officer replied in the same scoffing way—

" I should advise you to retain your present becoming civilian attire in which ladies find you so fascinating; but if you think otherwise, so be it."

With that he left them, and while one of the soldiers went for the uniform, the youth took the opportunity to say to Margaret—

" Allow me, mademoiselle, since I shall see you no more, to kiss your hand, and thank you."

Her hand he could kiss as she delivered it to him, but was not able to thank her, or not well enough; and before the words came the trooper returned, and he was led away. Margaret retired to her chamber.

All this while M. Meyer was in the lobby under guard, and as the German captain passed him, he said—

"So you have, it seems, a Frenchman in hiding here."

"Sir," answered the old gentleman, drawing himself up, "one of my fellow countrymen has honoured me by lodging here for the night."

"I have not asked your name."

"Meyer, at your service."

"A German name."

"So it please you, sir, I was born with that, but at the same time my hands, my tongue, my heart were born French."

"Are you a native of this place?"

"I was born a few miles away in Alsace."

"Elsass, old man, Elsass. But more of this hereafter; for the present you are free."

So saying he strode to the room set apart for him, while M. Meyer returned to the kitchen.

On their officer's withdrawal some of the Germans sat down quietly to their repast, but the rowdier spirits began at once to show

themselves, falling on the provisions like
beasts of prey. Sitting and standing, shouting, swearing and laughing, they guzzled
delicate wines and swallowed dainty dishes,
So far well, until the keenest of their hunger
was allayed, when they began to look about
them, disparaging the food with which they
were gorged, throwing morsels at the servants,
breaking bottles on the floor. A better trick !
One fellow seizes a shrieking wench by the
waist and kisses her ; another imitates him ;
a third does the same for Marie, the prettiest
of the maids, which Jean, with grinning
teeth, resenting, is knocked down by the
burly German. Now nothing will content
them, but to have all the kitchen sit down
with them, and partake their riot. The men
obeyed, some sullenly, some willingly ; the
women durst not refuse. So the uproar
grew until the quietest were infected.

M. Meyer had huzzaed when he heard of
the proclamation of war. His bold blood had
leapt up as in the days when he had himself
served his time, a bonny country lad. He
had boasted of Napoleon's name, and talked
of Berlin. He had hoped to see desolation

not settle on his own fair homestead but soar over the Rhine to billet her wolfish maw upon foes, who, when their goods were plundered, their houses defamed, their decency soiled, would—suffer like a Frenchman?

Something of this flashed across him, too swift for thought—a revelation, as he stood at the door and looked around him. Wasteful confusion everywhere afoot. The soldiers eating and drinking, holloing and stamping, breaking and spoiling, among the pale women; the table disgraced, the floor defiled; his own men joining the carousal; Jean with a bloody face, already drunk and embracing a fuddled Teuton.

Stepping forward with a stern glance and a beck he bade the women depart. All rose quickly but Mathurine, who forced to swallow glass after glass, lay now with her head on the table dead drunk. With many oaths the soldiers sought to retain the runaways.

"Sirs," spoke M. Meyer in German, loud and firm, "it is not the custom in our country for the women to sit drinking with the men. I pray you let them depart."

"No, no!" they shout; "the drabs shall

stay with us;" with things too brutal to rehearse. One blackguard, red with wine,
villanously treated a girl to his face. One
moment his heart stood still with indignation,
the next he had felled the culprit with one
mighty buffet. The man lay as still as a
log. The soldiers spring up, overturning their
seats.

"He has killed Hans Pfeiffer," they cry,
and in a twink have seized the offender.

"He has killed our comrade! Let us shoot
him!"

So they shout; and cursing, brawling,
struggling, force him out through the narrow
passage into the courtyard. Jean and his
fellows, sobered, stand together in dazed helpless amazement, while the women's shrieks
ring through the house, fetching down Margaret who was sitting upstairs in listening
dread, awakening the German officer who had
fallen asleep after his meal. The latter came
hastily forth, as his men, mad with wine and
fury, were hauling the old man along, and
roughly repulsing his daughter. His stern
commands were unheeded in the tumult.
Fiercely he approached, and kicking one,

striking another in the face, seizing a third by the throat, called out—

" Listen, fellows ! You shall repent this. What is this madness ? "

More subdued, but still retaining their captive, they cried—

" He has killed Hans Pfeiffer ! "

As they spoke, up staggered Hans, very drunk, but unconscious of decease.

" Here he is, you drunken ruffians ! Get you in, and let me have no more of this, if you value your vile carcases."

They slunk back into the house. Their captain turned with some slight excuses to M. Meyer, and was struck with the lovely figure that stood beside him. When he first saw her on the staircase by the lantern's dim light, he had little heeded her, but now in the bright daylight glistening on her face yet dewy with emotion, she seemed something of earth's best mould, heaven's choicest spirit. With a lower inclination and in stronger ex- pressions he regretted the disturbance, and then invited them both into his room ; a request which they might not refuse. In passing the kitchen they could see the troopers, some lying on the tables, some heaped against the walls and already snoring, some sitting moodily amid the ruins of their festivity. The servants had decamped, the fire was out.

Entering the parlour, Margaret and her father sat down with the officer. He asked them many questions, which they answered with the shortest civility; for their hearts were full and their tongues unready. However he had the more leisure to observe the maiden, and soon began to redouble his apologies, spoke of compensation and punishment, and would have put the chief offenders under confinement, but for Margaret's entreaties.

After a while the father begged his enforced guest to excuse his daughter's absence, who was worn out with fatigue, lack of sleep, and over-past excitement. Such a request could not be denied; and she having withdrawn, the officer thought again of his duties. He at once ordered the young Frenchman to be brought in. He enters in his military dress. The effort to stand upright in the enemy's presence has removed all trace of pain and weariness, except a paleness which may be indignation. The limp is away and he treads firm.

"Who are you?" asks the officer carelessly.

He is a French conscript serving as a private in such a division and regiment.

"Your name."

"Victor Cordon."

The German seems to be observing him more closely as he says—

"You were engaged at Worth?"

"I was."

"Where were you posted?"

The answer was given.

"I could not be mistaken; I remember cutting him down. You are the fellow who treacherously shot our captain after surrender."

"No surrender was made or thought of. We were few, but not afraid to die. I did shoot your commander, but honourably in open fight, as I would have done to twenty more had I been able."

"It is enough; I am my own witness. You shot my chief and friend against the rules of war, and you are yourself condemned to be shot by the rules of war. Take him out, Waack."

The lad was carried away, surprised but nothing daunted at the sudden sentence, trying hard not to think of his friends and home, and his young life that he had scarcely tasted, but to remember only his military duty and his country.

M. Meyer, when he had recovered from the shock, began to plead with the officer—

"For heaven's sake, sir, consider what you are doing. Shoot a young man whose only offence is to have served his country well!"

"Sir," replied the German stubbornly, "both by word and sign they offered to surrender, and when our captain, whom I succeed, cantered up to receive their submission, he was treacherously shot by that young traitor."

"There has been a mistake; he denies it."

"Doubtless he does."

"You have as much as acknowledged, sir, no offence to you, that we have received some injury; you have yourself spoken of compensation. I beg, I entreat—"

"Impossible, impossible," said the officer as he rose from his seat.

"By my grey hairs, by your warlike pride

X

and glory, by everything that is good on earth or in heaven—"

The officer had gone, and the old man was left writhing under the cruel dint of impotent pity.

Margaret in her chamber heard the stir in the yard below. Looking forth she beheld the young Frenchman led out. What now? See, he is pinioned, and placed by the row of poplars at the farther end of the court. Now the soldiers troop out of the house. Sharp short words of command, and they rank themselves just under her window. What does she hear? The order to load! Can it be that—? No time for the swiftest thought. In a moment she has flown the stairs and stands at the door. Too plain even to her ignorance what is afoot. Forgetting shame she flings herself at the officer's feet. He attempts to raise her. No; grasping his cloak she will there remain, until her broken words and sobs have gained the life. However touched, he is firm in his purpose, and since he cannot free himself from her grasp, turns his face away and gives the word—

"Present!"

No hope then? None; and she flings herself in despair on her young countryman's body. Fire now if ye will. The officer stepping up tried gently to disengage her. No, they should die together. It was impossible to remove her without extreme force, she herself being resolved, and her muscles as resolute as her will. The sergeant offers to assist, and even touches her, but is fiercely ordered back. What was to be done? The young Frenchman, weeping at last, himself in vain entreated her not to endanger herself. Should a base thing be sheltered by so precious a shield? Let him die, he did not fear; he was not so young as that. He should fall happy since she had deigned to regard him. But entreaty and threat were alike unavailing.

The captain looked at her and then at his men, but found no help. Again he looked at her, and if he was taken before with her bodily charms, now still more with her vehement courage. What wonder if he was glad enough to yield with some appearance of necessity?

Greatly moved, he said—

"He shall be spared, mademoiselle. Release him."

More intent on death than life she did not hear or understand.

"His life is given to you, only let me unloose your hand."

She heard, but doubted, until he said again more earnestly—

"I swear it by all that is sacred. Life and liberty."

So saying he bade them cut the youth's bonds. At last she believed, suffered herself to be removed, then fell to the ground.

The officer tried to raise her, and the French youth stooped to aid him. Which the sergeant again interfering would have prevented, but was stayed by a wrathful glance from his captain. Thus the two enemies, with little love between them, bore her into the house to her father, who was as much astounded at the bearers as the burden.

As soon as the young lady was deposited in safety, the German turned to Victor Cordon saying between his teeth—

"Go, and remember that your life and liberty are due to other merits than your own."

In vain his petition to stay even until Margaret revived. He was hurried away, and barely allowed to kiss his protector's un-

conscious hand and say a few words of thanks
to his generous host. When Margaret Meyer
regained herself he was a mile on the way to
Nancy.

*   *   *   *   *

Dreadful months followed. War swept
over the land carrying before it like a flood
things great and small; the little happiness
of a cot, the triumphant wealth of cities.
Weary months in which the sick watched and
the watchers also were sick. At last came
Peace, and flung her rich mantle over the
naked land.

What was sown in peace had not begun to
spring before the Meyers had an unlooked
for visit. A stately coach with bedizened
lackeys and noble horses drove to the door,
and out stepped a gentleman in rich military
uniform. He was admitted to M. Meyer's
presence, when he proved to be the German
officer who had stayed there on the night
after Worth. He was received hospitably, if
with no real gladness, and shortly began to
unveil his business, which was none other
than to sue for the hand of the fair Margaret.
With her at heart like a courageous amulet,

he had fought gaining promotion, and was then a colonel. Wealthy and of noble name, Baron von Propf returned with honours new and old, to claim the reward of his constancy, and his demeanour witnessed that he did not despair of success.

M. Meyer expressed his sense of the honour, but declared that he would not constrain his daughter's choice. The baron should speak for himself. Desiring nothing better he was at once ushered into Margaret's presence. To her he repeated the story with more eloquent amplifications, which the young lady heard patiently, and at the end replied—

" I thank you, sir, for this most honourable proposal, but there are several reasons why I must be bold enough to refuse it. In the first place I am a Frenchwoman, and as such will live, marry, and die."

He was eager to combat this position, but was at once stayed by her.

" I know what you would say, sir, but there are no arguments to change attachments, no reasons why a child should forget its mother. Moreover my decision has other grounds, in that I have this day been betrothed to another."

She tripped out, and in a minute returned upon the arm of a happy young man. The German saw at a glance that it was the same Victor Cordon whom he now regretted not to have shot. The two men saluted with no cordiality, and seeing matters stand so the baron was glad to take a short leave. The two lovers stood at the window and watched his coach rattle down hill.

*　　*　　*　　*　　*

When my friend Droit had finished, I clapped him on the knee, saying—

" Bravo, my dear fellow, a notable story. It proves your case completely—and mine also."

He returned some witty answer at my expense which I have forgotten, and then we both turned in to supper.

THE END.

Printed by REMINGTON & Co., 5, Arundel Street, Strand, W.C.

www.ingramcontent.com/pod-product-compliance
Lightning Source LLC
Chambersburg PA
CBHW031358270326
41929CB00010BA/1237